Anonymous

Sketch on the Causes of the Advance and Decline of Nations

with Strictures on Systems of Finance, Particularly Applied to Those of France and

Great Britain - Vol. 5

Anonymous

Sketch on the Causes of the Advance and Decline of Nations
with Strictures on Systems of Finance, Particularly Applied to Those of France and Great Britain - Vol. 5

ISBN/EAN: 9783337249809

Printed in Europe, USA, Canada, Australia, Japan

Cover: Foto ©Suzi / pixelio.de

More available books at **www.hansebooks.com**

SKETCH

ON THE

CAUSES OF THE ADVANCE AND DECLINE

OF

NATIONS;

WITH STRICTURES ON

SYSTEMS OF FINANCE,

PARTICULARLY APPLIED TO THOSE OF

FRANCE

AND

GREAT BRITAIN.

London:

PRINTED FOR THE AUTHOR,

AND SOLD BY J. JOHNSON, ST. PAUL'S-CHURCH-YARD; AND
DARTON AND HARVEY, GRACECHURCH STREET.

M,DCC,XCV.

ADVERTISEMENT.

From a conviction that it would be highly culpable, to delay giving any information on a subject, which the present aspect of public affairs renders more than commonly interesting; and which certain circumstances prevent me from entering into so fully as I had originally intended, or as its nature and importance demand; I have, in the following Sketch, attempted a discussion of its first principles: further illustrations of which, with those parts of the subject which have been unavoidably omitted, I propose laying before the public at a future period.

THE AUTHOR.

CHAP. I.

Introduction.

ALTHOUGH every species of inequality were unknown to men, in the early periods of society, yet in its progress towards civilization, in which the appropriation of lands and the partial accumulation of riches take place, we should discover the foundation of new and extraordinary changes, the difference of riches would begin to mark the difference of rank; by degrees, we should see different orders established, and at length completely formed the complicated mass, which society at this moment presents, in the civilized countries of the earth.

In this state of society, we discover that relation between the individual and the community, from whence arises the union of interests and exertions, by which the wants and desires of men are more abundantly supplied. But in this state, the proportion of the annual produce, which each individual enjoys, is by no means regulated

regulated by the degree of his industry or ability; as riches, while they remove the necessity of application, secure to their owner a much larger proportion of it.

To shew the nature of the circumstances necessary to this extraordinary production; and of riches, which give to many so large a part of it; together with the order of its distribution, which would take place in the natural state of things; and that most consistent with the general good of society, is the object of this work.

As our judgement of the other parts of this subject must be founded on the knowledge of the nature of stock, it, in the natural order, falls first under consideration.

CHAP. II.

Stock.

THE whole of the stock of the society is engaged in the three following employments; manufacturing, farming and mercantile; into one or other of which every possible manner of employing stock may be reduced. Under the title of manufacturing stock, we include the whole of that employed with the assistance of workmen, in the production of commodities, either directly, or in those employments which are necessary to others,

others, and of which they may be esteemed a branch. In the order of merchants, we include all those who purchase goods for the purpose of disposing of them, and stock thus employed we shall call mercantile stock.

The consideration of the nature and uses of these three divisions of stock, will divide this chapter into three parts.

PART I.

MANUFACTURING STOCK.

In the employments of men in civilized society, two circumstances are particularly to be remarked; 1st, That in very few cases labour is left unassisted; and 2d, that in no instance, the immediate productions of the workman are the rewards of his labour. In most cases also, before a commodity can be fitted for use, a very considerable time must elapse. In the mean time, the workmen must be supported. These circumstances point out the two necessary divisions of stock in every manufacturing employment. The first, called the fixed capital, and consisting of machines and other contrivances, for abridging labour. The second, called the circulating, which provides the wages of the workmen, and the raw materials on which they are employed, together with the subsistence of the manufacturer,

until

until the commodities, on which his workmen are employed, can be difpofed of.

The expences of the manufacturer, in erecting works, &c: are repaid, by being enabled to fave an equivalent in the production of his manufactures; as, by their affiftance, he may be enabled to produce a certain quantity of goods, with a proportionably fmaller number of workmen; and thus fave the whole amount of the difference of wages.

Improvements in the manufacturing art are, in general, made with fo much judgement, as not only to repay the manufacturer every expence, but alfo to enable him to fell his productions at a confiderably lower price, than thofe produced the ordinary way. As long as he can conceal the improvement, his profits are confiderably augmented. In fome cafes, the advantages arifing from fuch improvements are fecured, by patents, to the inventor for a certain time. This, independently of the encouragement which it very properly gives to ingenious men, is, in another point of view, no more than juftice; as it feldom happens, that a man, at the firft attempt, can put his ideas into execution, without committing fome miftakes. If, therefore, he were not fecured for fome time in the advantages arifing from his difcoveries, it would often happen, that in ferving the public he would fuffer materially;

rially; as others would profit by his failures. Improvements are often of a kind which muſt be concealed, in order that the advantages ariſing from them may be exclufively enjoyed by the inventor: of this kind me may confider improvements in the art of dying, &c. &c. The public, however, muſt, in the end, gain by all improvements, either on the expiration of the time for which the patent was granted, or by their being made public, which always happens fooner or later.

Strange as the affertion may at firſt fight appear, improvements in the arts are, however, lefs owing to the ingenuity of individuals, than the actual circumſtances of the fociety. In the courfe of this work, we fhall have occafion to point out the circumſtances which determine, at different times, the ſtate of manufactures with refpect to their different degrees of improvement, and to fhew, that a mode of manufacturing which, in one ſtate of fociety, would be attended by the moſt beneficial effects, would, in another, be attended by the reverfe.

In forming, therefore, a right judgement of thefe improvements, and their effects, we muſt compare the ſtate of fociety, with refpect to them, at different periods, and we fhall difcover, that although, at any particular time, they advance fo flowly as to be fcarcely perceptible;

yet, that they are certain and regular, depending on principles in their own nature fixed and invariable. It will be sufficient for our purpose, in this place, to remark, that the effects of these improvements are so great, even in but a moderate state of the advancement of society, that it enables the manufacturer, not only to advance wages sufficient to induce workmen to relinquish their usual employments, in which they enjoyed the whole produce of their labour, but also to sell his goods considerably cheaper than those produced by labour merely manual.

Until the manufacturer disposes of the produce of the labourers whom he employs, it is sufficiently evident, he must be out of pocket the whole amount of the wages advanced to his workmen, the value of the raw materials, and his own subsistence: the total amount of which will be either great or small, according to the number of workmen, the value of the materials, and the length of time necessary for the completion of the manufacture.

This part, or the circulating part of manufacturing stock, we see is necessarily resolved into the commodities of the ordinary consumption of the manufacturer, and of his workmen, together with the value of the materials on which they are employed. If these commodities did not exist in the society, no works could be undertaken which

which propose for their object the completion of manufactures at a remote period; as men would be under the necessity of employing themselves immediately in seeking subsistence.

That part of the manufacturing stock, necessary for the purchase of the raw materials, will be found to resolve itself into the same two parts; contrivances for abridging labour; and consumable commodities. The first, to occasion a great produce from little labour; the second, to feed, cloath, and provide, both the workmen and their employer, until the object of their labour is completed, and disposed of.

These materials, according to their different kinds, are either the productions of the farmer; as wool, flax, &c. or the productions of the stock and labour employed in mining, &c. Now, as the stock thus employed will be found to resolve itself into the same two portions, the materials produced by it may very properly be considered as also resolvable into the same two portions. If, for example, we suppose the person employed in the working of a copper mine, to work up the metal into all the various forms in which it afterwards appears, we should make no distinction between the stock necessary, in the first place, for working the mine, and that in the second, for providing the tools and subsistence of the workmen, for the further manufacturing the metal into the different articles, ready for comsumption. We should

should blend the whole under the two divions of which we have spoken; fixed, and circulating stock.

As society advances in improvement, the division of employments increases. The person who works the mine, frequently disposes of the ore. The extracting of the metal furnishes employment for a second; the working of the metal, to a considerable number; and, often, before the raw material appears in the form of an article fitted for consumption, it may have given employment to the stock, and labour of hundreds.

However inexplicable the real nature of the employments of men may appear, in civilized and in rich societies, we shall find, on reflection, the principles which regulate them, few and invariable. Perhaps, it would be altogether impossible to shew the proportions, which the parts of stock bear to each other, in the several manufacturing employments; nor would it, though it were possible, be at all to our purpose. For it is not our intention to shew the parts into which manufacturing stock, in a particular employment, may be resolved, but the parts into which the manufacturing stock of the society, taken in a mass, must, necessarily and unavoidably, be reduced. These parts are only two; machines, and other contrivances, by the assistance of which we are more abundantly supplied with the necessaries and conveniencies of life, and a quantity of commodities

modities sufficient for the consumption of the manufacturer and his workmen, till the objects of their labour are completed.

PART II.

FARMING STOCK.

Farming Stock is divided into the same two portions as manufacturing. Under the denomination of fixed capital, we are to consider implements of husbandry, and all improvements which tend, ultimately, to increase the produce of the land. The circulating capital provides the wages of the labourers, the subsistence of the farmer, and the feed, which may be considered, with respect to him, as raw materials, with respect to the manufacturer. Wages and the subsistence of the farmer are resolvable, also, into consumable commodities.

Thus, when we do not allow ourselves to be deceived by partial appearances, we discover the nature of both this, and the manufacturing stock of the society, to be extremely simple. We see a quantity of goods regularly consumed, and these replaced by labour. We must, also, easily perceive how great the quantity of consumable commodities, accumulated within the society, must be, which is sufficient to support the manufacturers, and the labouring part of the community, until the commodities, on which, at any moment,

labour

labour is employed, can be made ready for consumption.

In the anticipation of the rewards of labour, we observe a striking difference between the state of men, in civilized society, and those who derive a precarious subsistence from the chace. The subsistence of the Indian depends on the success of present exertion; while man, in a civilized state, draws it from the produce of former labours. That this takes place with respect to food, is too notorious not to strike every one; but a moment's reflection will enable us to discover, that it also takes place with every article of our consumption.

Hence an important and an unavoidable conclusion, that the inhabitants of any country can never be more numerous, than the commodities (under which we include food, and the other articles of common consumption) actually existing in the society can maintain, until the commodities, on which, at that moment, labour is employed, are finished and ready for consumption. Hence, also, as the quantity of the food, and other produce of the farmer, must depend on the state of the improvement of the lands, and his fixed stock, and on the number of labourers employed; and as the quantity of the productions of the manufacturer must also depend on his fixed stock, together with the number of workmen which his stock permits him to employ; so the state of the

population

population of every civilized fociety, is directly determined by the abundance of farming and manufacturing ſtock; that the population can never exceed what the lands in their actual ſtate of improvement, can maintain, is fufficiently evident; and that ſtock cannot increaſe without people, we ſhall afterwards more fully demonſtrate.

PART III.

MERCANTILE STOCK.

From local advantages, or from other cauſes, it frequently happens, that particular ſpecies of manufactures may be produced at a leſs expence in one country than in another, or even in different parts of the ſame country. Thoſe commodities, for example, to the production of which large quantities of fuel are neceſſary, will (other things being equal) be produced at a cheaper rate, in thoſe countries, in which fuel abounds, than in thoſe to which it muſt be carried at a confiderable expence.

In the many intermediate ſteps between that ſtate in which man ſtands alone, and that in which intereſt connects him intimately with others, there muſt have been a period at which a commercial intercourſe firſt began to take place, between places ſeparated from each other, which muſt neceſſarily have ariſen from the circumſtances above mentioned.

Hence

Hence arises the employment of the merchant, and the necessity of mercantile stock. This intercourse, however, is slow in its progress, and from the manner in which it gradually takes place, in a particular state, we shall be able to comprehend how it becomes more extended, and to see, distinctly, the limits to which it is confined, by the state of society at any one period.

Let us suppose that two places, London and York, for example, were supplied with all the articles of their consumption, by their own produce, (which at one period must actually have been the case;) but that, in York, a certain commodity was produced by less labour than in London; suppose woollen cloths: certain individuals must necessarily find an interest in purchasing cloths at York, in order to dispose of them in London. If the difference of price were great, the influx of this species of goods from York, would compel the manufacturer at London to employ himself in some other way; and London would in a short time be supplied with this article altogether from York.

If we suppose that, on an average, a space of three months is necessary, before these goods can be exposed to sale, in the London market, from the time of being completely out of the hands of the workmen at York, it must necessarily follow, that, if there be constantly at the London market, a quantity sufficient to answer the regular demand,

that

that a quantity of stock, precisely of the value of three months consumption of that article, is employed, over and above that which would be necessary, if London had been supplied by its own produce.

We may remark, by the way, that the time, in which it is possible to send goods from one place to another, will, by no means, regulate the quantity of stock which may be necessary; as the manufacturer must collect a certain quantity together, before they will pay the expence of conveyance: which is also, in general, very slow; as no commodities, except those of great value, and small bulk, can bear the expence of the quickest mode of conveyance; the advantage, arising from the quicker transmission, being more than overbalanced by the additional expence.

Thus, in addition to the commodities necessary for the consumption of the workmen and manufacturers, until the articles be finished, on which the labour of the society is employed, we see the necessity of a further accumulation, sufficient for the consumption of the society, until the articles of this kind can be procured from the places in which they are produced. These commodities belong to the merchant, and are called mercantile stock. The proportion which the mercantile stock may bear to the manufacturing and farming, will be determined by circumstances, to be treated of hereafter.

C H A P.

CHAP. III.

Of the Extent of the Market.

A CONDITION absolutely necessary to the extending the market, for the productions of any particular country, is, that it have some advantage by which certain goods may be sold as cheap, or cheaper, at a distant place, than those produced there; proper allowances being made for the necessary expences of transportation, &c. and the profits of the person who engages in such an employment.

In observing attentively the nature of the commerce carried on in any country, enjoying freedom of internal communication, we shall immediately observe, that in scarcely an instance, are the productions of any town consumed entirely by its own neighbourhood, or that it does not receive from some other place, part of the articles of its consumption. This must arise from the circumstance above mentioned, as in most countries, England for example, in which this freedom of communication is allowed, people enjoy a liberty of withdrawing their stock from one employment, and placing it in another, if they deem it of any advantage. If, therefore, goods be carried

ried from the north to the south, or from the east to the west, and after a great many expences, sold as cheap as those with which they may come in competition, it must arise from some very considerable advantage which one place enjoys over another, in the production of such commodities. In some cases, these advantages are altogether natural, from such, commercial intercourse must have at first arisen. But, in addition to these, we shall find another to which they give birth; we mean, the advantage arising from the division of employments, and which, in every case, depends on the extent of the market. This will be more fully explained in a following chapter.

Another condition, as necessary as the first, is, that the stock of the society be sufficient in quantity to allow of it. Whatever advantage one part of the country may have over another, in the production of certain manufactures, the extent of the exchange of commodities must be regulated by the quantity of the accumulation: for as the mercantile stock is employed in procuring, from one part of the country, those articles, in the production of which it may have an advantage; so the quantity which the merchant may find an interest in importing; or, in other words, the quantity of stock which he can thus employ with advantage, must be regulated by the quantity of goods which he can dispose of, or the value which he he can receive in exchange for them. In a very few inftances the merchant is paid for his commodities, by the merely natural productions of the country: the furs, for example, of North America. In this cafe, no degree of improvement or accumulation in North America is neceffary, in order to afford a more extended market for the productions of other countries. Such inftances however are rare, and we fhall find the quantity of goods, which people can purchafe, to depend, in general, on the commodities which they have in their power to give in exchange for them; and which, unlefs in a very few inftances, depend on the quantity of ftock employed in production. The commerce between two improved countries, or different parts of the fame improved country, confifts altogether in an exchange of manufactured commodities, or the productions of the farmer. As mercantile ftock, therefore, is employed in exchanging, and not in producing, it muft be more or lefs dependent on the other two branches of the general ftock. It will be found however to alter, in the proportion which its quantity may bear to the quantity of ftock otherwife employed according to the ftate of fociety, with refpect to improvement in the arts, and the quantity of accumulation on the whole.

CHAP.

CHAP. IV.

Of the Effect of the Extent of the Market on the Productive Powers of Labour, employed by Stock.

WHEN the stock of a country has become sufficient to allow of the three divisions, of which we have spoken, and when a greater quantity of a particular commodity is produced, at certain places, than that necessary for their consumption; a division of labour takes place, which will always be greater or less, in proportion to the quantity to be produced, or to the extent of the market. The following extract from the work of Dr. Smith, will sufficiently illustrate the effects of this division. "To take an example, (says he,) from a very trifling manufacture, but one in which the division of labour has been often taken notice of; the trade of the pinmaker. A workman not educated to this business, (which the division of labour has rendered a distinct trade,) nor acquainted with the use of the machinery employed, (to the invention of which probably the same division of labour has given occasion,) would scarcely, perhaps, with his utmost industry, make one pin a day, and certainly could not make twenty. But in the way in which this business is now carried on, not only the whole work is a peculiar trade, but it is divided into a number of branches, of which the greater part are likewife peculiar trades. One man draws out the wire, another ftraights it, a third cuts it, a fourth points it, a fifth grinds it at the top for receiving the head; to make the head requires two or three diftinct operations, to put it on is a peculiar bufinefs, to whiten the pins is another, it is even a trade by itfelf to put them into paper; and the important bufinefs of making a pin, is in this manner divided into about eighteen diftinct operations, which in fome manufactories are all performed by diftinct hands, though in others, the fame man will fometimes perform two or three of them. I have feen a fmall manufactory of this kind, where ten men only were employed, and where fome of them confequently performed two or three diftinct operations. But though they were very poor, and therefore but indifferently accommodated with the neceffary machinery, they could, when they exerted themfelves, make among them, about twelve pounds of pins a day. There are in a pound upwards of four thoufand pins of a middling fize. Thofe ten perfons, therefore, could make, among them, upwards of forty thoufand pins a day: each perfon, therefore, making a tenth of forty thoufand pins, might be confidered as making four thoufand pins a day.

But,

But, if they had all wrought feparately, and independently, and without any of them having been educated to this particular bufinefs, they certainly could not each of them have made twenty, perhaps not one pin a day; that is, certainly not the two hundredth, and perhaps not the four thoufandth part of what they are at prefent capable of performing, in confequence of a proper divifion, and combination of their different operations."

From this we may form a very good idea refpecting the effects of a judicious divifion of labour, and which will always be in proportion to the quantity of a certain commodity to be produced, or to the extent of the market. In many other employments, as the fame author obferves, a divifion of the fame kind takes place, but being, from the magnitude of the works, or from other caufes, divided, fo as that a few only of the operations can be perceived at one time, it is much lefs evident.

In this inftance, however, we have feen the divifion of labour, only as it tends to produce a greater quantity of goods, by a proper application of it. But we may go further, and fee a divifion take place, which involves the ftocks of hundreds, and the labour perhaps of many thoufands. We fhall take one inftance only, which will fufficiently illuftrate this point. In the working of a me-

tallic

tallic mine, the stock of an individual, however great, is often trifling, compared with that necessary for even drawing the ore from the earth. We frequently see companies formed for this purpose, and even their united stocks, are altogether insufficient for working up the metal into manufactures. This forms employment for the stocks of others, who give it, perhaps, another aspect, when it is handed over to a third; and, as we have formerly observed, the metal may pass through the hands of hundreds, before it appears in the form for which it was originally destined. Were we to conceive the whole of the stock, which is thus divided amongst so many, in possession of one person, or company, they must be determined by its quantity, in the manner of employing it, and the proportions of it, which might with advantage be employed in each stage of the process, from the procuring the metal from the mine, until it was completely manufactured. Were too great a quantity employed, in the first stages of the process, it must incapacitate them from working up the whole of the metal, and the stock, employed in procuring the superabundant quantity of the material, would prove wholly unproductive. As a man who would, with a stock of £500, set about building a house which required £2000, he must stop after he had got the foundation laid, and his stock would be little better than thrown away.

We

We are not to conceive, however, becaufe this divifion of ftock takes place, that the nature of things are altered, or that no relation exifts between the parts of ftock in the feveral employments. The term *demand*, fo well known amongft merchants and manufacturers, is a demonftrative proof, that this relation does exift. The perfon who works up the metal into the common articles of confumption, is determined by the quantity of thefe articles, for which there is a demand; the perfon, who extracts the ore, is determined in the quantity which he purchafes from the miner, by the quantity of the metal he can difpofe of; and the miner alfo, is determined in the quantity of ftock he can employ with advantage, by the quantity of the produce for which there is a demand. Of this, however, we fhall treat more particularly hereafter, where we fhall place the nature of demand, in a new point of view.

The divifions of ftock, which take place in the production of certain commodities, it is fufficiently evident, muft be regulated by the quantity of the commodities, for which there is a demand. If the market, however, were confined to a particular town, or its neighbourhood, but a very trifling part of this divifion could take place; and it may be doubted, if any manufactures, but thofe of the moft fimple and homely kind, would ever, be eftablifhed.

Nothing contributes so much to the extending the market, for the productions of particular places, as the establishing of good roads and canals. The advantages which arise from them, will scarcely admit of calculation: for when we observe certain articles sold at a cheaper rate, in one part of the country, than in another, we are not to compare the difference of price, with the expence of making a communication, because those articles, which could not bear the expence of ordinary carriage, may very well bear the charges attendant on a conveyance by water; and by the market becoming more extensive, greater divisions of labour and stock may take place in their production; and consequently may be sold at a price still lower.

CHAP. V.

Of the Extent of the Market, as it affects the Manner of the Employment of Stock.

IF we suppose a country excluded from all foreign intercourse, the divisions which take place in its stock, and the manner of its being employed, must be regulated by its internal consumption, and as the communications between the several parts of it are more or less easy.

But, when commerce takes place between different nations, the consumption of the one has a considerable effect on the productions of the other. If the commerce of England were solely confined to itself, its stock would necessarily be employed, in the production of articles for its own consumption; but if, in this state, a connection were suddenly opened with another country, France suppose, we should see a very material change in the products of England; many of these would find a market in France; and many of the products of France, would find a sale in the markets of England. The importation of French commodities into England, and of English into France, would necessarily alter the common course of the demand. Certain manufactures in
England

England would, perhaps, be annihilated, by the influx of goods from France: the fame would happen in France, by the influx of goods from England. Many workmen would be thrown out of employment in both countries, and, as they are feldom addicted to philofophizing, would perhaps, deem their deftruction inevitable.

The future effects of fuch a communication are well worth attending to. After the commerce between the two countries had got into a regular courfe, as the demand had been increafed in each country for certain fpecies of goods, the ftock and labour thrown out of one employment, would find it in another: the fame ftock, the fame labour, would ftill be employed, though in a different manner. The inconveniences attending this freedom of intercourfe would be only temporary, and, which is particularly deferving of notice, the greater the diftrefs of the workmen, on the abolition of commercial reftrictions, the ftronger the proof of the neceffity of fuch an abolition, as it demonftrates the poffibility of a more proper application of ftock.

The advantage accruing to the two countries, England and France, from fuch a freedom of commerce, would be, in the firft place, the difference between the price of the commodities imported into each country, compared with the price of fuch commodities before the communication;

-cation; (not to speak of new productions unknown to each country before) and in the second, a further reduction of their price, as greater divisions of stock and labour took place in their production.

If we carry our views but a little farther, we shall discover, that the more extended the foreign commerce of any country is, the fewer must be the species of its manufactures. If we compare the number of the species of manufactures, in a particular town, with the number in the whole country, or with the different kinds of commodities consumed within the town, we shall find the former bear a very small proportion to either of the latter. But when we also compare the *quantity* of the commodity or commodities produced within that town, with its consumption of these same commodities, we shall observe a very striking difference, which will be either greater or less, in proportion to the extent of its commerce, with the towns and country in its neighbourhood.

The nature of foreign commerce, and the manner in which it enriches nations, is simply by affording a more extended market for the productions of each, by which, in each nation, the quantity of commodities may be greatly increased, in consequence of the greater divisions of stock and labour.

Commerce between nations is precisely of the same kind, with the exchange which takes place between individuals, after the division of employments has been established; and, as in this case, the more he is confined to a particular and simple operation, the more it tends to the good of the society of which he is a member; so in that, the more simple the labours of any particular society, and the more it confines itself to the production of but a few commodities, the more it tends, not only to the good of that individual nation, but also of every other with which it is connected.

A notion is commonly entertained, that by admitting the manufactures of other countries, we discourage our own. No doubt we do, of that particular species of manufacture; but it must be considered, that our manufactures of another kind are, exactly in the same degree, encouraged: because the goods imported, must be paid for by an exportation: and, in every case, we cannot have a more certain proof of a great exportation, than by a great importation. An importation, without an exportation, can take place, only when foreigners come over with their stocks, for the purpose of settling; (which is acknowledged to be of considerable advantage;) nor can an exportation take place, without an importation, except when people leave the country, for
the

the purpofe of fettling in fome other; which is as generally allowed to be of difadvantage.

Thus far, this reafoning has ever appeared fatisfactory: but it has been the opinion of many; that importation of goods is attended, in many cafes, by the exportation of money. The late celebrated Dr. Smith has endeavoured to prove, that this opinion is altogether groundlefs; and that the quantity of money, circulating in a country, can be leffened or increafed, only by other methods; and that importation or exportation of goods, in the ordinary courfe of trade, do not affect it, as one muft balance the other. We fhall afterwards have occafion to enforce the opinion of the Doctor in part, and to point out fome circumftances which regulate the quantity of money, of which he does not appear to have been aware.

CHAP.

CHAP. VI.

Of the Division of Stock.

Every individual wishes to engage his stock in the most profitable employment; but, as in every employment, not more than a certain quantity can be engaged with the common advantages, it will be necessary to point out the manner in which stock is engaged under different circumstances, consistently with the interest of individuals.

The state of the society, with respect to improvement in the arts, and the quantity of the accumulation on the whole, will determine the quantity which may be engaged with advantage, in each of the three employments.

As every species of stock must have arisen originally from labour, it would at first be employed in assisting it. Stock, therefore, would at first be employed in manufacturing and farming. Mercantile stock can never stand alone, as its business consists, in assisting the exchange, not in the production of commodities. It is, consequently, at all times, dependent on the other two branches of stock. The proportion, however, which

which it bears to them, is very different at different times.

When an individual finds that, by importing goods, either from foreign countries, or diſtant parts of the ſame country, he may increaſe his profits, he naturally employs his ſtock in doing ſo; and as the ſtock of the ſociety becomes ſufficient to admit of numerous diviſions of labour, and when the productions of particular places are conſumed at a diſtance, the quantity of ſtock, neceſſary to be employed in exchanging, muſt be increaſed. As the market for the productions of every particular part of a country becomes extended through the whole, ſo muſt the mercantile ſtock be increaſed, in order to admit of it, and thus gradually begins to bear a greater proportion to the other two parts of the general ſtock.

In order that very great diviſions of labour may take place, it is often only neceſſary, that all the ſtock and labour, employed in the production of a certain commodity, be got together in one place. The ſame ſtock, with the ſame, or a ſmaller number of workmen, may produce a much greater quantity of goods. Expenſive works, which facilitate the production, may be erected with advantage, when a great quantity of a particular kind of goods is to be produced. When a great quantity of a particular article is

manufac-

manufactured at the same place, it also happens, that the stocks of five or six different people, are concerned in the complete manufacture of it. No division of stock, of this kind, can take place, where a small quantity only is to be produced, although we were to suppose the individuals equally rich, and that each employed the same number of workmen. For, in considering the full extent of the division of stock and of labour, we are not to confine ourselves to remarking the quantity of stock and the number of workmen employed, by a certain manufacturer; we must take into consideration, the stock and workmen employed by others, on the material, in its different aspects, and form our judgement from a view of the whole.

But, as the more an individual is confined to a simple operation, the more he becomes dependent on the other individuals of the society; so with particular towns or nations; and, as a certain degree of accumulation of commodities is necessary, before labour can be applied, in a manner which is not immediately productive; (which we have already shewn to be the case with all employments in civilized society) and, as the abundance of this accumulation must determine the degree of this division of labour; that is, whether labour shall be employed on commodities which require six, twelve or eighteen months, &c. to their production;

tion; and, as in treating of mercantile stock, we have shewn that, when a commerce takes place between distant places, a still greater quantity of goods is necessary, than those, of which the manufacturer has the command; so the divisions of stock and labour, which take place in manufacturing, are as directly dependent on mercantile, as manufacturing stock.

Thus we see that, in different countries, or in the same country, at different times, the most advantageous divisions of labour and stock will be regulated by the abundance of this species of riches. Under improper circumstances, great divisions of labour would be highly destructive: like a man who sailed on a three months voyage with provisions on board but for two.

From the premises, we may conclude, that the quantity of mercantile stock, in proportion to manufacturing and farming, is always greatest, when the market for the productions of particular places is most extensive.

The manner in which these divisions of stock take place, and their effects on the revenue of the society, will be easily understood. The object of every manufacturer and merchant, is, to increase their profits. The manufacturer attempts it, by improving his machinery, &c. the merchant, by procuring goods at the cheapest market: but as improvements in manufacturing, and the cheapeſt market become known, they are obliged to lower their prices, until their profits are on a level with thoſe of others. As there were never two places alike in every circumſtance, it will generally happen, that commodities may be produced, at a cheaper rate, in one place, than in another; that is with leſs labour. It does not happen, however, that manufactories are always eſtabliſhed at the places beſt adapted for them. A proper diviſion of labour, and a knowledge of the art, may give to certain places an advantage over others, which enjoy very conſiderable natural ones: but when certain places obtain an advantage over others in the production of particular goods, from whatever cauſes it may ariſe, whether from a natural or acquired ſuperiority, ſuch places muſt acquire a ſtill greater, and open to themſelves a more extended market, in conſequence of the diviſions of labour, which follow the greater demand.

A mere difference of price, is not, however, the only thing which can determine the degree of the extent of the market. The greater the diſtance between two places, the greater muſt be the difference of the price of particular commodities, in order to allow of an extenſive commerce. The profit of the merchant muſt depend on the additional price which he can lay on each article imported; which, in order that his profits may be on a level with thofe of others, muft be determined by the time in which he can turn his ftock. A merchant with a ftock of £5000, which he turns twice a year with a profit of 5 per cent, is on a level with him who, on the fame ftock, which he turns but once a year, has a profit of 10 per cent.

But as the diftance becomes greater, and as each place becomes more dependent on others for the articles of its confumption, fo the quantity of mercantile ftock increafes: thus, in a ftate advancing in improvement, the manufacturing and farming ftock increafe, but the mercantile in a ftill greater proportion. This is the natural order in which ftock divides itfelf in the progrefs of fociety, that is, the divifion which individual intereft will always tend to promote; for, if this increafe of the mercantile ftock did not take place, or if we were for a moment to conceive it fuddenly leffened, we fhould perceive the profits of the merchants confiderably increafed. It fometimes happens, from unexpected interruptions in the ordinary courfe of commerce, that the articles of a certain kind at market are infufficient to fupply the demand. In this cafe, the dealers in thefe articles enjoy a temporary monopoly; or, in other words, the mercantile ftock is infufficient. The profits of the merchants are, therefore, for the moment, augmented. If any means could be devifed to prevent ftock from being employed as mercantile, when the profits of this particular employment were increafed, merchants would enjoy a conftant monopoly of this kind.

As neither the merchant, nor his ftock, is employed directly in production, it follows that it can only be augmented in two ways; 1ft, by the profit of the merchant; or, 2d, by ftock, which had been accumulated in the other two employments, being converted into mercantile ftock. But, as competition reduces the profit in all employments nearly to a level, the firft will be infufficient to account for the greater increafe of the mercantile ftock in the progrefs of fociety. We, on the other hand, feldom fee people withdrawing their ftock from one employment, to place it in another, which is always attended by confiderable inconvenience. The proportions, between the feveral parts of ftock, we fhall find preferved more generally by the choice of profeffions. A parent, whether farmer, manufacturer, or merchant, wifhes to place his children in the moft profitable employment, which, while a fociety is advancing, muft be the mercantile. Thus we frequently fee part of the ftock, which had been accumulated by the father, in the manufacturing or farming employments, engaged by the children in the mercantile.

From

From the great quantity of mercantile stock in rich societies, which is never employed in production, and on every portion of which the merchant expects a profit, it might, at first view, be supposed, that the revenue of the society, or the quantity of consumable commodities, annually produced, is not increased in quantity, in proportion to the numbers amongst whom it is to be divided. But, from what we have already said, it will be sufficiently evident, that, although mercantile stock is not immediately employed in production; yet the divisions, which take place in the other employments, are dependent on it; and as the object of these divisions, is to increase the produce from the same labour, which can be be marked, only, by the fall of the price of each article thus produced; and as the merchant, after these improvements, is able to sell his goods cheaper, than those on which the wages of labour and the profit of the manufacturer, only, are charged, after allowing himself the ordinary profit on his whole stock; so these improvements which depend on the mercantile stock, are not only sufficient to allow of the profit on its greater quantity, but more than sufficient; which may be known by the difference of the price of those commodities at different times. Of this, however, we shall treat more particularly hereafter.

It muſt indeed be acknowledged, that the intereſt of the lower orders is not immediately forwarded by theſe diviſions of ſtock and labour, and the conſequently greater increaſe of mercantile ſtock. The abundance of their wages depends on the increaſe of the manufacturing and farming ſtocks. If ſtock, as it was accumulated, was employed in production, the demand for labour would increaſe along with it: did this, however, take place, the revenue of the ſociety would never be ſo great as if freedom of commerce were allowed. In the former caſe, wages would quickly riſe; but never to any great height. In the latter, they riſe more ſlowly; but in the courſe of ſome time are much more conſiderable; becauſe, the revenue, or the productions ariſing from the labour and ſtock of the country, always increaſes, as the accumulation of the ſociety approaches to that ſtate, which admits the greateſt poſſible diviſions of labour. This alſo we ſhall treat more particularly of, when we come to ſpeak of the diviſion of the revenue.

CHAP.

CHAP. VII.

Of the nominal Value of Commodities.

THE revenue of every individual is dependent on the price of some commodity or commodities. The rent of the landlord depends on the price which the farmer receives for the produce of the land. The wages of the workmen and labourers, employed by the manufacturers and farmers, together with the profits of the latter, are secured by the price at which their several productions are sold. The profit also of the merchant depends on the difference between the price at which he purchases, and that at which he sells.

From these facts, the late Dr. Smith has concluded, that the price of all commodities is determined by the price of the produce of the land, (by which rent is ultimately regulated) the price of wages and profit. These he calls the component parts of the price of commodities. The price of commodities, therefore, according to him, must rise or fall with the rate of any or all of these species of revenue.

This mode of reasoning is, at first sight, extremely plausible, but, on a close examination, will be found totally unfounded. For commo-

dities do not bear a certain price, *becaufe* wages of labour, profits of ftock, or rent of land are at a certain rate; but becaufe the whole of the produce muft be diftributed amongft the three orders of which fociety is compofed; landlords, workmen, and owners of ftock, (from whom every other fpecies of revenue is derived) and as the diftribution is made by each order charging a certain nominal value on the different productions, as they pafs through their hands, fo, unlefs they bore this value, the proper diftribution of the revenue could not be made. This will be beft illuftrated by an example. Let us fuppofe two focieties, each confifting of fifteen families, and each confined to itfelf: let it be fuppofed that, from particular circumftances, three families in the one were neceffary to fupply the whole fociety with food and raw materials for manufactures; while, in the other, two only were fufficient to provide the fame quantity. The quantity of finifhed commodities, to be devided in the one muft, therefore, exceed the quantity to be divided in the other. If this divifion be made through the medium of money, and each perfon charge a price on the commodity which fell to his fhare to produce, in proportion to his labour, it muft neceffarily follow, that the individuals of the one fociety, in difpofing of their productions amongft each other, muft, in o der that the produce of
their

their united labours be equally divided, either fell the manufactured goods dearer than thofe in the other, while the price of the raw materials and food is the fame in both; or, while the price of the manufactured goods is the fame in both, purchafe their raw materials and food at a greater. In every ftate of fociety, the revenue of the individual muft depend on the difference between that which he gives and that which he receives. When money ferves as the medium of all exchanges, the nature of things remains the fame; the only difference is, that people then fpeak of the prices only of things. If, in thefe two focieties, the price of food, &c. be raifed in confequence of its reprefenting not only the quantity of labour employed in procuring it, but rent alfo, ftill the manufactured commodities muft be fold at the fame price. The rife in the price of the produce could only affect the revenues of thofe employed in manufacturing (which we may call profit or wages) but could not in the fmalleft degree raife the price of manufactures. After ftock has been accumulated, and its divifions with that of labour eftablifhed, the fame principle holds. If certain articles be rifen in price, either in confequence of more labour becoming neceflary to procure them, or a rife in the revenue of certain orders, it is altogether impoffible that it can be compenfated by the rife of

thofe

those goods on which the revenues of the other orders depend.

The causes of deception on this subject, are chiefly two. 1st, The unequal rise or fall in the value of several sorts of rude produce. 2d, The alterations which take place in the distribution of the revenue. We shall afterwards have occasion to shew that the profits of stock must fall in the progress of society towards improvement, attended by the rise of wages. In this place, it is not our business to shew how these changes take place, but to confine ourselves to a view of their effects on the nominal value of particular commodities.

If every portion of rude produce were to rise in value in such a manner, as to affect each employer of stock exactly alike, we should see them sell their commodities at the usual price, while they were obliged to pay an advanced one on the material; but as it is altogether impossible that each owner of stock can be affected exactly alike, so unless the value of the articles produced in certain employments were raised, the rise in the price of the material must fall on an individual. But although, by the rise of one species of revenue, (rent) we see particular commodities raised in value, yet commodities in general cannot be in the least degree affected; the whole mass at market must bear precisely the same value. The rise of rent will fall on profit and wages, and as much

much as particular species of commodities are raised by the advance of the former, others will be sunk by the depression of the latter*.

The

* As, at first view, it does not appear evident why the rise of the materials of one species of manufacture, in consequence of the rise of rent, attended by a rise of the articles into which such materials enter, should occasion a depression of the price of other manufactured articles; we subjoin a further illustration for the perusal of those who are more than ordinarily inclined to abstract enquiry.

The stocks of the manufacturers, merchants, and farmers, anticipate the three species of revenue; rent, profit, and wages. The greater the proportion which one order receives, the less must be that of some other. If the manufacturer, therefore, give a greater price for raw materials, he makes over to the landlord part of that which had represented his own profits, together with the wages of his workmen: unless, therefore, he lessens his own expences, the whole amount of the advance of the price of the material, it is very evident, he cannot employ the same number of workmen, at the ordinary rate of wages, nor produce the same quantity of goods. There would still be in the society the same quantity of materials, and the same number of workmen, but the commodities which had represented profits and stock being lessened, must compel workmen to take less wages. As the diminution of the quantity of commodities, (or which amounts to the same thing, as the money which had given the manufacturer the command of these commodities, had been handed over to the landlord,) had been made in one employment, there would be a necessity of a new distribution of stock and labour, amongst the several employments, in order that the same quantity of goods should be produced in each, and an equality of wages and profit preserved. The stock which had been engaged in purchasing

and

The reader must recollect, that in this place, we speak only of the value of goods, as affected by the different species of revenue, and the value which one article must bear, when compared with another, in order that the revenue shall be distributed. The circumstances which determine their absolute value, or the quantity of gold and silver

and working up the materials, which retained the same value, would, in consequence of the reduction of wages, be sufficient for the purchase of an additional quantity of materials, and the employment of a greater number of workmen. While the stock, in the other employment, in consequence of the increased price in the material, would be insufficient for the employment of the usual number. We should therefore see a quantity of stock turned from one employment into another: different quantities of stock, in consequence of this change in the distribution of the revenue, becoming necessary to produce the same quantity of goods. And thus, if we suppose profits of stock to remain the same, the reduction of the rate of wages must enable those, in the employments not affected by the increased value of materials, to lower the value of their goods. The reduction of the rate of wages must also keep down, in some degree, the price of those goods whose materials were raised. If the increase of rent be supposed to affect profit, the effects on the nominal value of goods will be precisely the same; one article will be raised in price, and another reduced in precisely the same proportion; the reduction of one species of revenue always attending the increase of another.

Hence, it will appear, that the staple commodities of a country, will be different at different times, according as rent of land, profits of stock, or wages of labour predominate.

for

for which they shall exchange, will be treated of hereafter.

When the profits of stock are reduced, and wages of labour raised, certain goods must be affected in value, some must be raised and others reduced. According to the value of the materials and other circumstances, the quantity of stock necessary to give employment to a certain number of workmen, must vary; but if wages were raised in every employment, while the nominal value of goods was kept stationary, the owners of stock in the different employments, must be very differently affected; those who with a great stock employed a certain number of workmen, must suffer much less than they who with a smaller stock employed the same number. Competition, however, would oblige the one to lower the price of his goods, while that of the other, in order that he should enjoy the common profits, must be raised.

In a word, to judge rightly of the manner in which the nominal value of goods is regulated, we must not confine ourselves to a partial view. If the reader will consider, that the whole of the annual productions is parcelled out amongst the different orders of which society is composed, either as rent of land, wages of labour, or profits of stock, and that this division is made by commodities bearing a certain price, consistently with the

the circumstances already pointed out; he will, at a single glance, perceive the changes which must take place, in the prices of certain commodities, under different circumstances.

CHAP. VIII.

Accumulation of Stock.

WHEN we consider the nature of stock, as consisting of an accumulation of commodities, employed either in setting labourers to work, or in procuring manufactured goods from distant places by exchange, it will be readily seen, that when the quantity is sufficient for these purposes, in their greatest possible extent; to wit, when in every employment, the greatest possible divisions of labour may have taken place; which require, as we have already shewn, a proportionably greater quantity of mercantile stock, every further accumulation, we say, must be more equally divided, amongst its three divisions of manufacturing, farming, and mercantile.

Stock, however, in its own nature, is inert and unproductive, even in manufacturing and farming

ing. It is not the stock which produces, in these employments, but the labour, which, in consequence of accumulation, may be more advantageously applied. When the divisions of labour are as great as possible, and when every increase of mercantile stock must wait the increase of the other two parts of the general stock; the increase of the whole must be attended by a proportional increase of people. To work up double the quantity of raw materials, double the number of people is necessary; nor is it possible to conceive the further augmentation of the one, without that of the other. It may indeed be carried from one country to another, but if the stock, already in the country, be sufficient for the purposes enumerated, a quantity, equal to that introduced, must remain somewhere unemployed; either the manufacturer must want workmen, or the merchant turn his stock more slowly. It may not, however, be the stock thus introduced, that remains unemployed; if the person who possesses it, wishes to employ it in manufacturing, he has only to give greater wages than ordinary to procure workmen; or if he employ it as mercantile stock, he has only to shew a little more taste than common in the choice of his goods, or to sell for a lower price, to procure customers. It requires, however, a very considerable increase of stock, even in a particular employment, to produce the least

sensible

sensible effect, as it must be proportioned to the quantity of the superabundant stock, when compared to the quantity necessary in the employment. Perhaps at no time, is the quantity in each, neither more nor less than that necessary; as it is impossible to form an accurate idea of the circumstances on which it depends. The profits of stock are never exactly the same in all employments; sometimes they are higher, and at other times lower. These variations are owing to the quantity of stock, in each employment, being sometimes more, and at other times less, than that necessary.

When the people of a country are as numerous as the spontaneous produce of the lands can maintain, every further increase of the population must depend on the accumulation of stock in the several employments. The quantity of commodities, of which the farmer has the command, must determine the number of people which he can employ; the produce of their labours must, also, repay to him his advances. The labourers employed immediately on the land, are not the only ones, who derive employment and subsistence from the stock of the farmer. The higher the state of cultivation, the fewer hands are necessary, when compared with the produce. We must consider, however, the number of hands which have been employed, in getting

the

the lands in a ſtate to admit of it, and the number neceſſary to keep them in it. The maſons that have been employed in erecting the neceſſary buildings, walls, &c. the manufacturers, alſo, employed in making the inſtruments of agriculture, &c. The workmen employed in each manufacturing employment, muſt, alſo, depend on the ſtock of the manufacturer, who is alſo repaid for his advances, by the produce of their labours. Were we to conceive the whole of theſe commodities, which are diſtributed as wages of labour, and as the ſubſiſtence of the owners of ſtock, in the hands of one perſon, the number of people, which they were capable of ſupporting, muſt neceſſarily be determined by their quantity; he muſt diſtribute them in ſuch a manner that, as any particular article was conſumed, it ſhould be replaced by the produce of thoſe to whom he had advanced ſubſiſtence. If it took, on an average, ſix months before the articles could be finiſhed, on which labour was employed, the number of people which they could maintain, muſt be greater, than if twelve months were neneceſſary, and juſt in proportion to the difference in time. If the farmers of Great Britain could produce two crops in the year, each as abundant as the ordinary one; if manufacturers could produce goods in one half the time at preſent neceſſary; the ſtock at preſent in Great Britain

Britain could give employment to twice the number of people with equal eafe. The accumulation of confumable commodities, is not, however, the only thing neceffary; it is alfo neceffary, that the land be in fuch a ftate, as to be capable of producing a quantity of food and other produce, within a given time, equal or greater, than the confumption within the fame period; this depends on the fixed ftock. The fame muft take place in every manufacturing employment. When the whole annual produce is confumed, without a view to a reproduction, as the quantity of commodities remain without any increafe, the inhabitants muft remain ftationary, with refpect to their numbers. We fhall afterwards, point out fome very material differences produced by the manner of confumption.

The very great effects of improvements on the land, and in manufacturing, muft be fufficiently evident, on comparing the annual produce and population of two countries together, in which different degrees of thefe improvements take place. The lands in the interior parts of America are, perhaps, as fertile, and enjoy as many natural advantages, as thofe of Europe; yet, the inhabitants are not in the proportion of one to a thoufand, and are even, for their numbers, much worfe fupplied with the neceffaries and conveniencies of life.

An

An improved agriculture has nearly the fame effect in producing food, as improved machinery, in the production of manufactures; the effects, perhaps, are not fo great, they are, however, confiderable. It is obferved by Dr. Smith, who has taken fo much trouble in collecting the prices of corn, that its value is in general nearly the fame, in Poland, France, and England. In the latter, however, the rent of land, compared with the extent of the country, is much greater, than in either of the former; this greater rent, the farmer is enabled to pay, by his produce bearing a certain price: but this, it feems, is fo much increafed, on the whole, in confequence of improvements, that the price of each particular portion is not affected. In China, fuppofed to be the moft populous country on earth, the price of food is confiderably lower, than in any part of Europe, which muft arife from its being produced by lefs labour than in other places, in confequence of a more improved manner of cultivation, and a divifion of the lands, into fmall portions, the effects of which we fhall fhew hereafter.

An effect of accumulation, has been fuppofed, the reduction of profit, and the nominal value of goods. We have already fhewn, that the reduction of one fpecies of revenue, can affect the nominal value of goods only partially: with refpect to the reduction of profit, which always takes place,

place, it muſt be attended by an equal increaſe of the revenues of either the landlord or the workmen. While the revenue on the whole remains ſtationary, every depreſſion in that of the one order, muſt be attended by an equal riſe in that of ſome other; if the revenue on the whole increaſe, it muſt be attended, either by the riſe in the nominal value of the revenue of each; or, while this remains ſtationary, the depreſſion of the nominal value of goods. It is in this latter way, that improvements in the arts ſerve ſociety. The greater the quantity of every ſpecies of goods, produced by the labour and ſtock of the ſociety, the lower the nominal value of each article muſt be; and this increaſe of the quantity produced, directly ariſes from accumulation. The fall of the nominal value of goods, in general, can be, by no means, owing to the fall of profit; becauſe, as much as the value of goods was lowered by the depreſſion of profit, it would be raiſed by the riſe in ſome other ſpecies of revenue.

As ſtock, ſays Dr. Smith, may increaſe in a particular employment, beyond what may be employed with advantage, ſo may it increaſe in every employment. The Doctor, it is evident, drew the general concluſion, from the particular fact; but, although ſtock may increaſe in a particular employment, unattended by the uſual advantages, it is abſolutely impoſſible, that it can increaſe

in

in the fame manner in all employments. The quantity of ſtock, employed in a particular way, is regulated, only, by the quantity of the whole; it never is but a relative quantity, if the quantity of ſtock be doubled in every employment, with the fame increaſe of workmen, things muſt be preciſely as they were; with this difference, that as the quantity of goods, to be produced, is doubled, greater diviſions of labour may take place in each employment; and thus, in a ſhort time, the annual produce may be more than doubled. Six people may produce a quantity as 4, but tweve may produce a quantity as 9 or 10.

We have already ſhewn that, in the progreſs of a ſociety in riches, a greater increaſe of mercantile ſtock takes place, than of manufacturing and farming; and conſequently a greater increaſe of ſtock than of people; but even in the manufacturing and farming employments, an increaſe of ſtock takes place, in a ſmall degree, without an equal increaſe of workmen, on whom manufacturers and farmers are more immediately dependent. All improvements in machinery, &c. are made with a view of becoming leſs dependent on the workmen; but, as in conſequence of theſe, the competition among the workmen keeps wages at nearly their uſual rate, and, as other people, alſo, employ their ſtocks, as it accumulates, in procuring goods from other places,

places, inſtead of employing workmen immediately in production; ſo we ſee the neceſſity of a greater increaſe of ſtock, than of people, and the profits of the owners of ſtock, kept up above what they would fall to, if the introduction of machinery and foreign commerce, or commerce between diſtant parts of the ſame country, were prevented. But although every increaſe of ſtock is not attended by an equal increaſe of people, in the progreſs of accumulation; yet, as it approaches to that ſtate, which (as we have formerly obſerved) admits of the greateſt poſſible diviſions of labour, and when ſtock cannot be increaſed in the mercantile employment, without being alſo increaſed in the others, the increaſe of people muſt bear a greater proportion to the increaſe of ſtock; and when it has arrived at the degrees above mentioned, every increaſe of the one, muſt be attended by an equal increaſe of the other. When this takes place, the revenue of the ſociety, compared with the number of people, muſt be at its greateſt height. The manner of diſtribution, in the mean time, undergoes ſome change, wages of labour riſe, and profits of ſtock fall; but wages of labour riſe in a greater degree than profits of ſtock fall; becauſe, the quantity to be divided gradually increaſes. In the diviſion of revenue, there are ſome other circumſtances to be pointed out, beſides

sides these, which will be remarked in the course of the work.

When we consider the manner in which accumulation takes place, we shall find further proofs of what we have advanced. Accumulation, it is generally supposed, takes place, when those who derive a revenue, either from their land or stock, spend less than their income. The person who thus adds to his riches, may either hoard up his savings, or employ them himself, or lend them to those who will. If the profits of a merchant, who has a stock of £5000, amount to £500 per ann. and he expend but two hundred, he may lay by £300 yearly, and thus at the end of ten years, he will have accumulated the sum of £3000; but if, in place of hoarding it up, he employ it, he will receive a profit on it, as well as on his original capital; and thus, at the end of the same period, his capital will be of a much greater value, than had he allowed his profits to remain unemployed. In the one case, it accumulates like simple interest, on a certain sum, in the other like compound.

In the present state of society, in which, no one is under a necessity of concealing his wealth, the practice of hoarding is almost altogether unknown. The passion which, in one state of society, urges a man to conceal his treasure, in another, induces him to employ it, by which he is known to be possessed of it. If society got rich by hoarding; the productions of former ages muſt make a very confiderable part of the wealth of every fociety; but if we take this into view, we ſhall perceive, that almoſt every part of it, has been the produce of the preſent year ; or at moſt, of the two or three preceding it (we ſpeak here only of ſtock.) If we look at the various productions of the manufacturer and farmer, the almoſt infinite variety imported by the merchant, we ſhall find, that they are almoſt all intended for immediate confumption, and that no part has been the produce of former ages, or is intended for the uſe of future. That focieties do not get rich by the hoarding of money, is alſo abundantly evident. The expences of the American war amounted to about 170 millions ſterling, a value which no perſon ſuppoſed exiſted in Great Britain, as money; much lefs, that the money in Great Britain was diminiſhed that amount. If the wealth of a fociety confiſted in money, the wealth of every individual ſhould, alfo, lie in it; but if a man, who fays he is worth ten thouſand pounds, be aſked how much money he has, on an average, in his poffeffion, he will moſt probably fay a fum not much exceeding two or three hundred pounds.

When we compare the increaſe of the people in America, with the increaſe of thofe in Europe, we ſhall be ſtruck with the difference, but as, in accounting for this great increaſe of

people,

people, we should be wrong in ascribing it to their longevity; so, in accounting for the increase of wealth, we should be wrong in attributing it to hoarding, either money or commodities. In every case, we shall find, even in those countries advancing fastest into wealth, that the whole of the annual productions are consumed.

In the manner of consumption, we are, therefore, to look for the causes of the increase of wealth. Every species of consumption, may be reduced to two; that with, and that without, a view to reproduction. The quantity of the annual produce consumed in the one way, when compared with the quantity consumed in the other, must at all times regulate the degree of the advance of society in riches. When farmers and manufacturers save a part of their profits, and employ labourers with it, the whole of their profits is as regularly consumed, as if they had purchased with it articles for their own immediate consumption. In the one case, it is consumption without, in the other, with a view to reproduction. The profits thus employed, are reproduced, and increase their stock, and consequently their ability of employing workmen. If landlords save from their revenues, although they do not employ it themselves; yet, by lending it to others, to which they are prompted by their interest, the effects on the increase of wealth and population

pulation is the fame. The more œconomical farmers, manufacturers, merchants, and landlords, the higher muſt be the rate of wages, to enable the lower orders to rear up families, in order that the increaſe of people may attend that of ſtock. While the ſtock of the country remains unaugmented, if an increaſe were to take place in the number of its inhabitants, part muſt ſtarve, or the whole be ſatisfied to receive leſs wages than ordinary. But, although, from rigid œconomy, the lower orders might be enabled to bring up more numerous families, than they do at preſent; yet, unleſs accompanied by a certain increaſe of ſtock, it would be rearing up their children to inevitable miſery. If the wages of the parents were low, thoſe of the children muſt be ſtill lower. The powers of generation are not the only limits to the increaſe of the human ſpecies. When the infant enters into life, unleſs it meet with nouriſhment and ſupport, it neceſſarily returns to nonexiſtence. If a manufacturers ſave £500 from his income, the number of people which he can employ, will be increaſed, juſt in the proportion which the ſaving bears to his capital ſtock. If the ordinary rate of wages, however, had been (as it at preſent is in moſt of the countries of Europe) no more than ſufficient to enable the workmen to continue themſelves (if we are allowed the expreſſion;) or, if the

population

population be stationary, in order to obtain the additional number, he must bid against others, which must raise the rate of wages; this competition must be either greater or less, in proportion to the degree of œconomy amongst the several orders. If the same manufacturer, in place of saving £500, save £700, he must require a still greater number of people to put it in motion, and consequently the competition for workmen becomes still greater. Thus we see the natural order, from great savings, arise great wages; from great wages, numerous families. The happiness of the greater part of mankind, also, depends on the accumulation of stock, which, by keeping up their wages, gives them a command of a greater share of the annual productions of a country. We call that the profit of the manufacturer, or farmer or merchant, which they either consume, or add to their stocks; but how different are the effects of each. In the one case he lives for himself alone; in the other he is only the steward of the public. By establishing a fund for the support of a greater number of people, he may with justice consider himself, as not only the author of the happiness of multitudes, but also of their existence. The effects of profits saved, and of profits spent, on articles of immediate consumption, are so different, that they should not be known under the same name.

In

In societies advancing in wealth, we shall find another difference, besides that of consumption, when compared with those stationary or declining; namely, a difference in production.

CHAP. IX.

Of Production, as determined by the State of Society.

WE have already shewn, that stock, in allowing those numerous divisions of labour, which are so beneficial to society, anticipates the revenues of those orders, from which arise every species of revenue. We shall see, however, that it also anticipates, in many cases, the revenue of those, who it might appear at first sight, derive no revenue, until the productions of their land or stock, have repaid all the expences which had been advanced. We may comprehend, landlords and those who lend money on interest, in this order. The landlord does not expect to be paid his rent, until some time after the tenant may have held possession of the land, nor the person who lends his money on interest, till the expiration of a settled period, when it may be supposed the person to whom he has lent it, has actually derived

derived some advantage from it; but the landlord, in disposing of the rent of his land, and the money-lender of the interest of his money, will purchase goods, which perhaps have been produced a number of months, or even two or three years before. The money, which the manufacturer or merchant borrows, is employed, perhaps, either in the production or purchase of goods, which are sent to Spain to purchase gold or silver; the gold or silver purchased with these commodities, sent to China or India, to purchase teas or muslins; and before the article purchased by the produce of his stock may arrive, perhaps two or three years, or even more, have elapsed; at the moment, however, the landlord receives the rent of his land, or the money-lender the interest of his money, they may command these commodities as certainly, as if they had been immediately produced on the lands of the one, or by the stock of the other.

It will evidently appear, therefore, that commodites are not produced in consequence of the immediate demand for consumption, into which every species of demand must finally be resolved. The Indian, who weaves the muslin, may say he has a demand for it, but we trace this to the European purchaser, and find that it is ultimately regulated by consumption. It will follow then, that as production is not in consequence of the
immediate

immediate demand for confumption, it muft be regulated by experience, or the fuppofition that there will be, at a diftant period, the fame demand for a certain article that there is at prefent. The farmer, when he fows his wheat, does it with perfect confidence, that as people have eaten, fo they will alfo at a future day. It happens, however, that in many cafes, people are under the neceffity of employing their ftocks on mere conjecture; this is the cafe with thofe who are engaged in producing articles of fafhion, who always muft fuffer, if the demand fall fhort of their expectation. Demand is, however, frequently affected by other circumftances than a mere change of fancy, and when the ordinary courfe of it meets with confiderable interruption, it is then called a ftagnation of trade. This always takes place, when the productions of one country are excluded from the ports of another, in which they had ufually found a market: but as it happens that the confumption of nations, lying near each other, is pretty much of the fame kind, the articles produced for foreign confumption, find, in the courfe of fome time, a market either at home or in fome other country. Thefe interruptions, however, muft always be attended by confiderable lofs; in the firft place, as a greater quantity of ftock had been employed in the production of certain fpecies of commodities, for which the demand

mand had ceafed, until thefe commodities are fold, the fuperabundant ftock in particular employments, is wholly unproductive, the manufacturer, who can employ workmen only by felling his goods, muft be altogether incapacitated from employing any for fome time; and, in the fecond place, after thefe goods are fold, the manufacturer is obliged to turn his ftock into fome other employment, of which a perfect knowledge may be fuppofed wanting, and in which ftock cannot for fome time be very profitably employed: to thefe we muft add the lofs of the fixed ftock, neceffary in the former occupation, and which, it is more than a chance, may be ufelefs in the latter. Workmen will alfo for fome time be thrown out of employment, as well of others, as of thofe now become ufelefs; for the ftock, in confequence of a fudden interruption of the ordinary courfe of the demand, will be conveyed to other employments, which it would appear were wholly unconnected with thofe, in which the interruption had originated. The demand for food appears to be one of thofe which nothing could interrupt; but if we fuppofe the manufacturers of Birmingham and Sheffield, for example, employed in fupplying the market of France, as well as of England, with hardware, and in confequence of a war, the communication deftroyed, we fhould fee a quantity of a certain fpecies of goods,

greater

greater than that neceffary for the fupply of the home market. The workmen would be thrown out of employment, nor could they for fome time find it in any other; but the power which they have of purchafing food, as well as other articles of confumption, muft depend on the regular payment of their wages. Thus the farmer, and every perfon who employs labourers, muft be affected, and exactly in proportion as a greater or fmaller fhare of the national induftry, is forced from one channel into another. As ftock is turned from the old channel, the bad effects of the interruption begin to difappear, and when it has got entirely into the new, are no more to be obferved.

The worft effects of an alteration in the common courfe of the demand, are therefore, the immediate ones; which are always bankruptcies, and workmen thrown out of employment. Bankruptcies may take place, although the merchant or manufacturer be poffeffed of a confiderable ftock, if they cannot difpofe of it. It will fcarcely admit of doubt, that many of the firft trading houfes, both in Great Britain and Ireland, would have become bankrupt, had it not been for the affiftance afforded by the governments of each country, which muft have been followed by the fall of leffer ones; as it is well known in the mercantile world, that many fmall houfes depend for their credit on one great one. In a word, the
connection

connection between the several parts of a trading state is so intimate, that what directly affects one, cannot fail of indirectly affecting the others, and that, (as we have before observed,) according to the degree of the original interruption.

We see, therefore, that the *kind* of the productions of the society, on which labour is employed, is regulated by the demand for consumption, at the moment; and that the commodities at any time at market, will be of the kind for which there may have been a demand, whatever the demand may be at that moment.

When the manufacturers, farmers, merchants, or landholders, in place of purchasing articles for their own immediate consumption, employ workmen, (which must take place whenever accumulation takes place ; no matter where, for if it accumulates faster with the merchant than with either of the other orders, part of it must be turned from the mercantile employments, in order that the equilibrium be preserved ; or, if it takes place with the landlord, he lends it to some person, so that in every case it must go to the employment of labour,) the demand, we say, for the commodities of the ordinary consumption of these orders, no longer exists in the same degree. The stock and labour usually employed in producing them, become useless, as great part of the goods must remain unsold. Were a sudden change of

manners

manners to take place; that is, if landholders and the owners of stock, had ordinarily spent their whole revenues, in purchasing articles for their own immediate consumption, and were suddenly to become œconomical, we should see an effect produced, of much the same kind as that we have been describing. We should see an interruption in the ordinary course of the demand, attended by its concomitants, bankruptcies and want of employment for workmen. In the course of some short time, they must however find it, in the employments in which the demand had been increased, and as the goods were disposed of in a foreign market, for which the demand at home had ceased, the stock would be employed in some other way. Thus, after things had got into a regular course, we should observe the demand of the manufacturer, increasing from year to year, for raw materials, and other things necessary in his employment; and as a greater number of hands would be necessary, from year to year, the wages of labour must rise, in order to allow of their increase. Thus we should observe the demand of the manufacturer, only, altered. The stock and labour, which had been employed in producing the articles which he had generally consumed, and for which the demand had ceased, would be employed in raising materials, and in supplying the market with other articles necessary for manufacturing,

nufacturing, and in furnishing the articles of the extraordinary confumption of the workmen. It is often afked, what would become of the numerous workmen, employed in manufacturing the articles of the luxury of the rich, were the demand for them to ceafe? We anfwer, that their being thus employed, is amongft the principal caufes of that extremity of wretchednefs, under which the lower orders of mankind groan in Europe; were they not employed in adminiftering to the vices and follies of the great, they would be employed in manufacturing articles of neceffity and convenience for themfelves. It is falfe, that luxury is no evil in a commercial ftate, for it directly ftrikes at the prefent happinefs of the greater part of mankind, and prevents the poffibility of their future increafe.

According, therefore, as the fociety is advancing, ftationary, or declining, fo will a greater or fmaller proportion of the induftry of the country, be employed either in producing articles which ferve as the foundation of a reproduction, or employed in producing articles to be confumed, without the poffibility of any.

In focieties advancing the fafteft in riches, a greater proportion of the labour and ftock is employed in producing food and materials, and tools neceffary for manufactures; that is, in agriculture and the ufeful manufactures. Hence,

F

other things being equal, the society advancing the fastest in wealth and population, will have the least foreign commerce. In this state of society, the lower orders consume a great proportion of the annual produce, and the different classes of men are œconomical.

In societies stationary, the annual production of commodities, for the consumption of the lower orders, is only sufficient to allow the race to be continued. In this state of society, the different classes of men spend the whole amount of their revenues.

In societies declining, the production of the commodities, for the consumption of the lower orders, is not sufficient to allow the race to be continued. In this state, a man who marries, entails inevitable misery on both himself and his posterity; it will therefore be avoided. In this state, men spend either more than their revenues, and consequently encroach by degrees on their stocks, or when they have acquired large fortunes, they leave the country, as in the British possessions in India. In such societies, the diminution of the stock, is attended by a diminution of the number of inhabitants, till at length they are not more numerous, than the spontaneous produce of the land can maintain. Hence in societies stationary and declining, there will necessarily be a greater *shew* of riches. A greater proportion of
their

their inhabitants, will be in towns. The stock and labour, which should be employed in procuring the means of subsistence for a rising generation, will be employed in the production of luxuries; for the use of a few. Foreign commerce will flourish at the expence of agriculture, and the ornamental manufactures, at the expence of the useful.

Many authors have spoken of the decline of nations, as a thing inseparable from human affairs, and appear to think it as inevitable, as the approach of old age, and, at length, dissolution to man. But society, in the mass, can never be compared with the individual. The causes of the advances or decline of the former, we may discover and remove; but of those concerning the latter, we are totally ignorant. To prove the necessity of a dissolution of society, we must prove the soil less fertile, we must prove the decline of the mental and bodily faculties of man.

The slow increase of most of the nations of Europe, in wealth and population, and the decline of some, we shall shew to arise from two causes, not necessarily connected with the present state of society, and the effects of which have been wholly misunderstood.

CHAP.

CHAP. X.

One of the Causes of the slow Progress of Europe, in Population and Riches.

IN no case, does the history of man furnish us with an instance of so rapid an increase in wealth and population, as that presented to us by the United States of North America. If we compare it with the advances made by the countries of Europe, we shall be struck by the immensity of the difference. One of the causes of which, we think, may be found in the law of entail, so common in Europe.

When we compare the expences of men of large landed properties, with their revenues, we shall find, that in place of contributing by œconomy, their proper share to the increase of the society in wealth and population, they directly prevent it. It will scarcely admit of doubt, that the expences of landholders are, in general, greater than their incomes; else, why so many estates mortgaged, or why are they so often to be sold? Nothing is more common, than to see people of small fortunes, leave to their children, five, six, ten, or even more times the sum, of which they had originally been possessed. But who

who ever faw a fortune of £40,000 a year doubled; or if fome favings are made from fo large a revenue, they are applied to the purchafe of the eftate of fome fpendthrift. When a man of landed property fpends more than his income, it is as deftructive to fociety, as when a manufacturer encroaches on his ftock. The demand in both cafes, is increafed for goods to be immediately confumed, without hope of reproduction. If a landholder run in debt to the amount of five thoufand pounds, that is, if he confume goods to that amount, more than his revenue allowed, he may make over part of his eftate to his creditors, and thus replace to them the part of their ftock which he had confumed; but, there muft ftill be five thoufand pounds worth of goods in the fociety, lefs than there would have been, had he confined himfelf to his income. The particular manufacturer or merchant, may not fuffer by his extravagance; but the effect on the population and wealth of the country, is juft the fame, as if they had deftroyed that portion of their ftock.

But, by the law of entail, a revenue is raifed from the other orders of the ftate, which, were it not for this law, would remain with them, and confequently increafe their ability of accumulation. If we afk the reafon of the low price of corn in America, we are anfwered, that as the people have no rent to pay, they may afford to

F 3 fell

sell their produce at a considerably less price. We would ask, what would be the difference between Europe and America in this respect, if the law of entail were abolished, by which, in the course of half a century, or a little more, estates would be so much divided, as to oblige their possessors to become their cultivators! There could be none. The necessity of œconomy to those possessed of small fortunes; the prevalence of manners contributing to encourage it, would together conspire to increase the wealth of the society, accompanied by an equal increase in the numbers, and in the happiness of the lower orders of the people. The person who is both the owner and cultivator of the land, must always have an interest in improving it, as he is certain of enjoying the advantages both of the landlord and the farmer. The rapid increase of stock on the land, in consequence of the œconomy attendant on small fortunes, must, in a short time, increase the annual productions to such a degree, as to sink every particular portion of it considerably in value: the ability of accumulation on the land must be lessened, and the profits of the stock employed on it, at length, approach nearer to the profits of stock in other employments.

These changes would, however, be attended by others of the greatest importance; by the fall of the price of provisions, labourers on the ordinary, or on less wages, would be enabled to rear up more numerous families; the expences of the owners of stock may be reduced, and thus, their ability of accumulation increased, so as to attend the increase of population. In a word, a law which would abolish that of entail, might truly be considered as the agrarian law, which would give to the meanest citizen, an immediate and direct interest in every portion of the land of the state.

But the baneful effects of the law of entail, may be traced much further. Men of large fortunes give the bias to the manners of the people; thus, we see a spirit of expence pervade every order of men, where the aristocracy is considerable. Every man leaves his own station, to appear in that above him. From a pride which makes every one unwillingly acknowledge a superior; what he cannot be, he endeavours to appear. Nature, for important purposes, has established in man, a constant desire for action. In every situation of life, there is some object, to which he bends his desires and exertions; but the actions of men in society, are never indifferent, they must produce some good, or some bad effect. Is it not then particularly incumbent on us, that we discover, if possible, the circumstances under which these desires may be exerted, so as to become useful? The citizen, in promoting his own interest, we see diffusing plenty and happiness; the monarch, desolating nations, and entailing misery on posterity*. From whatever causes those circumstances arise, which remove from certain individuals the necessity of applying themselves in a manner which may be useful to society, they must pervert the natural order of things; we may consider them as not only the source of many of the miseries of mankind, but also of the vices. Amongst these causes, the law of entail stands most conspicuous.

In some instances, we see the owners of large fortunes, animated with public spirit: in times of distress they afford some assistance to the lower

---

* " Nobility is not hereditary in China."—" However illustrious any man has been, nay, though he had been raised to the highest dignity of the empire, the children, whom he leaves behind, have their fortune to make, and if they have not a great deal of spirit, or love their ease, they sink to the rank of the vulgar, and are often obliged to follow the meanest profession: it is true, that a person may succeed to his father's possessions, but not to his dignity or reputation; he must rise by the same degrees as his father did."

Du Halde.

" There are four sorts of professions, say the Chinese philosophers, absolutely necessary in the empire, which are sufficient for providing necessaries, and maintaining good order, viz. that of the learned, that of the husbandmen, that of the mechanics, and that of the merchants."

Du Halde.

orders; but the man who gives even a tenth part of his income in charity, is scarcely known. But although such instances were more general; yet, the very exertion of this generosity, supposes injustice: were things in their natural state, that is, the state consistent with public and private justice, (for the law of entail is an equal violation of both,) it would be out of the power of any class of men, to offer any considerable assistance to another; nor would there be any need of this assistance, as the lower orders would enjoy that as their *right*, which they so very seldom receive from courtesy *.

* " The present European communities, (says a warm supporter of the rights of mankind,) appear to be all more or less infected with prejudices, not easily eradicated, arising from the unnatural and feudal classification of states into nobility, clergy, burghers, peasants, &c. The whole community, except the two first classes, are called *Roturiers* in France, *Commons* in Great Britain, and *Ofrelse*, (that is *unsafe*,) in Sweden. These distinctions appeared to have encouraged pride and idleness in the first class, bigotry and intolerance in the second, and to have increased the misery and poverty of the whole last class, who form, however, the greatest part of the state."

WADSTROM's Essay on Colonization, § 606. (3.)

C H A P.

CHAP. X.

Of the Accumulation of Stock on Land.

IT must be evident, that no part of the rent of the landlord, which is derived from the employment of stock on the land, is employed so as to increase its produce. To every increase of stock on the land, and consequently production, we must look to the savings of the farmer. If the farmer sold his produce, at market, at a price no more than sufficient to repay himself for his expences, with his usual profits, it must be evident, that stock might increase on the land as fast as in the ordinary way, in which the price of the produce, must not only repay the farmer for his expences, but must enable him to pay a certain rent to his landlord; but, by so great a fall in the price of provisions, workmen would be enabled to rear more numerous families; merchants, manufacturers, &c. by a reduction in their expences, would be better enabled to accumulate; there must soon be a demand for provisions, and other kinds of produce, which so slow an increase of stock on the land could not supply. The quantity being smaller than that for which there was a demand, must occasion a rise in its price, which,

by

by raifing the profit of the farmer, muft enable him to fupply the market, as plentifully as the demand required. If things be left in a ftate into which they would, of their own accord, fall, it is abfolutely impoffible, that fo effential an article as food can be wanting, as the moment the quantity is leffened, the price is raifed, which permits a greater produdion; and the moment the quantity is increafed beyond the regular confumption, the price muft fall, which, prevents more ftock and labour from being employed, than what at any time may be neceffary.

The nature of ftock, which has been laid out on the land, is, in fome circumftances, different from the ftock in other employments, from which it will more generally happen, that the market muft be overftocked than underftocked. From the moment, ftock has been employed in draining, inclofing, erecting buildings, &c. it is funk in fuch a manner, as never afterwards can be withdrawn. If the lands be fold, the purchafer has the fame intereft in making the moft of the improvements. In many manufacturing employments, and altogether in the mercantile, ftock may be withdrawn from the production or importation of certain fpecies of commodities, to the production or importation of others. Merchants and manufacturers have it alfo in their power to remove their ftocks altogether from the country,

country, which is by no means the cafe with the farmer. Although the annual production of food, and other kinds of produce, exceed the annual demand or confumption, yet, it muft be the intereft of every farmer, to raife as much as poffible from his lands, on the quantity of which his profits muft depend, whatever the quantity be neceffary for the regular confumption. If the quantity of the confumption of a fociety be as 50, and this be furnifhed by a number of people as 25, each perfon will furnifh a quantity as 2; but, although the confumption fhould remain at 50, if one of thefe 25 be able to increafe his production of 2 to 3, his profit muft be increafed, and juft in proportion to the increafe of the quantity; as, although the whole quantity of 51 fold for the fame fum as the quantity of 50; yet his particular profit muft be augmented, as his produce would always fell for half as much more as the produce of any other perfon, that being the difference in quantity.

In everyemployment, manufacturing as well as farming, it muft always be the intereft of the individual, to increafe his produce as much as poffible; and thus, by the neceffity of exertion becoming general, each is more plentifully fupplied with the articles of his confumption. Combinations fometimes deftroy the good effects which muft arife from this general neceffity of exertion;

exertion: thefe are in every cafe hurtful to fociety, as well thofe into which men of particular employments will enter, if allowed, as thofe allowed, and fometimes countenanced, by government, as corporations, &c.

The fuperior advantages of ftock employed in the land, to ftock otherwife employed, have been by fome authors much infifted on, who think it particularly behoves government to encourage this mode of its application; but this is an abfurdity. After a certain quantity has been difpofed of on the land, to lay out more muft not only be ufelefs but unprofitable. If more provifions be raifed than may be neceffary to fupply the confumption, of what importance, we would afk, or of what ufe, is the fuperabundant quantity? would not the ftock and labour employed in procuring it, have been much better employed in raifing other articles of confumption? That the quantity can never be lefs than to fupply the demand for confumption, is fecured, as in the manufacturing employments, by the intereft of individuals; as, whenever the quantity is leffened, the price is raifed, which gives encouragement and ability to increafe the produ&ion. In the natural order of things, the price of provifions, &c. muft always enable the farmer to increafe his ftock, and confequently his produ&ions, in the fame degree that ftock increafes in other employments.

ployments. The increase of stock, in both, being attended by an increase of population.

In countries, where the lands are divided into small portions, as the price of provisions must be lower, than in those where the law of entail takes place, it will happen, that the demand from other countries must raise the price above that which would generally take place, if exportation were prevented. Thus the demand for corn has always been considerable in North America, which must have kept its price above what it would have been at, had the production been regulated by internal consumption. The increase of price in this way is, however, not attended by those baneful effects, occasioned by the high price, in consequence of the law of entail. Whatever the profits of the farmer may be, while he continues to save them, there must be an increase of the population. If the great emigration from Europe has not kept down the rate of wages, they must have been raised with the price of provisions. By this emigration, the labouring part of the community must suffer little, as it either reduces the rate of their wages, or keeps it stationary, while the price of provisions is raised, in consequence of the increased demand, occasioned by the present situation of the nations of Europe. The extraordinary rise in the price of provisions in America, must be owing, in a great measure,

to

to the fuddennefs of the demand; fhould the fame demand continue, the great profits of the farmer muft, in a fhort time, enable him to raife a quantity fufficient to fupply the foreign demand, as well as internal confumption, at a lower price. While the farmer enjoys moft of the advantages arifing from the foreign demand, merchants and manufacturers muft fuffer a little, in confequence of their expences being increafed, and by the rife of the wages of labour, unlefs as we have already obferved, they be kept at their ufual rate, by the emigration from Europe. All the advantages of the American farmers we fhall find, however, only temporary, and we fhall fee his profits, the moment the nations of Europe get into a fettled ftate, fall as much below mediocrity, as they are at prefent above it; for the great demand muft induce him to increafe his produce by every means in his power, he muft put himfelf to more than an ordinary expence (which he is enabled to do by his extraordinary profits) to increafe it as much as poffible. But whenever foreign demand ceafes, or is leffened, the price of every portion of his produce muft fall to a price confiderably lower, than that neceffary to enable him to increafe his ftock, as faft as it increafes in other employments. His profits muft be lower than ordinary, until the increafe of ftock and in other employments and of population, allow of the confumption of the whole of his produce; his profits will then rife to a level with the profits of others and (if we are allowed the expreffion) he will ftart from a new goal. While the price remains lower than ordinary, merchants, manufacturers, &c. will enjoy more than their proper fhare of the annual productions, as in the other cafe they muft enjoy lefs; particularly manufacturers, as the reduction of the price of provifions may enable the labourers to take lefs wages. The benefit arifing from a reduction of his own expences he muft enjoy in common with others.

We have here fuppofed the alterations in the price of provifions to affect merchants and manufacturers nearly equally; but, perhaps, this is not the cafe, as the effects muft be only temporary. As wages of labour are a good deal regulated by the price of provifions, and as the manufacturer is more immediately dependent on workmen, than the merchant, he muft neceffarily be more affected. Great differences of profit cannot indeed take place fo long between manufacturing and mercantile, as between thefe and the farming employment. In the courfe of a fhort time, the merchant can turn the whole of his ftock into the manufacturing employment. As the value of it is conftantly coming into his hands in money, he has only to ftop purchafing, in order to have it

in

in a form the moſt convenient for applying it, as may ſeem moſt for his advantage. The manufacturer, alſo, may turn in a ſhort time his ſtock into mercantile, without much loſs. But as the farmer never receives the whole of the value of his ſtock in the ordinary courſe of his buſineſs, when he wiſhes to change his employment, he muſt ſell it for what at that moment may be made of it, which is ſeldom regulated by what it coſt him. Changes, however, from one profeſſion to another, are, as we have before obſerved, but ſeldom made, except when great interruptions in the ordinary courſe of trade, make them abſolutely neceſſary, and are then more or leſs ſubject to inconveniencies.

G CHAP.

CHAP. XII.

Of Demand, as it affects the Quantity of Production.

IF we take into view, only the fact, that with every individual, the quantity of commodities which he produces, and the quantity of stock which he can employ with advantage, in a particular manner, must depend on the demand; we might conclude, that there are certain circumstances, which regulate the quantity of commodities produced on the whole. But when we consider the quantity of the commodity produced or imported by the individual, as a quantity relative to that produced on the whole, we shall reject this opinion, and consider demand, what it really is, a necessary attendant on production. Although the demand of the society, is, at all times, regulated by its productions, which it never can exceed, and which it at all times must accompany; yet, at any particular moment, the demand must have as great an influence in determining the quantity of stock, which can be engaged with advantage in a particular employment, as if the demand was totally independent of production. If we suppose, that one of two nations was exactly twice as populous and twice as rich as the other, their confumption confifting of the fame fpecies of commodities; it muft follow, that there would be a twice greater demand, and twice the production for a certain article, in one fociety, than in the other. It might, however, be very poffible to produce or import into the minor fociety, as great a quantity of a certain article as in the major: but this, it is evident, muft be contrary to the intereft of thofe who would thus employ their ftocks. It is neceffary, therefore, to diftinguifh between demand, as it relates to the individual, and as it relates to the fociety.

In a former chapter, we have had occafion to remark the alterations which fometimes take place in the demand, and confequently in production: but demand can never regulate more than the fpecies of production; of the quantity of production, it is properly only an afpect. While there is production, there muft be demand; nor is it poffible to conceive one without the other *. From what we have already faid, we believe the reader will find no difficulty in perceiving the

* To fuppofe that there may be a production of commodities without a demand, (provided thefe commodities be of the right fpecies, and no individual can have an intereft in producing any other) is as abfurd as to fuppofe, that the revenues of the feveral individuals compofing the fociety may be too great for their confumption: indeed the former fuppofition neceffarily includes the latter.

truth of the proposition. We shall, however, examine the effect of hoarding money on demand and production, which appears least favourable to what we have advanced. In the present day, it almost never takes place; but, in pointing out the effects in this view, it will serve to remove every doubt. If any set of men were to lay up the money, which represents their share of the revenue, in place of employing it in the purchase of goods; it is evident, that the quantity in circulation must be diminished, by degrees, and unless supplied from a new source, must in the end wholly disappear. We have then to ask, would it be the interest of any set of men to make up the deficiency in the circulation? We say it would; and that equal to the quantity hoarded up. In this place, we shall take for granted, what we shall demonstrate more fully in another chapter, That the value of money depends on its quantity. Money is an article of such small bulk, as to be easily conveyed from one country to another, in which it may bear a greater value. It accordingly serves as the medium of exchange, as well between different countries, as between the individuals of the same country. The merchant, who exports the productions of Great Britain to Portugal, sells them at a certain price, and the merchant, who imports the productions of Portugal, purchases them

them at a certain price. Thus, the interest which the merchant of one country has in importing the goods of another, muſt be always determined by the price at which he purchaſes, and that at which he ſells. This neceſſarily confines the commerce, between two countries, to the importation and exportation of certain commodities only, in the production of which one may have, over the other, either a natural or acquired ſuperiority. This ſuperiority, in production, muſt alſo be great enough, to allow the expences attendant on conveyance, &c.

It is not the buſineſs of the merchant, however, to conſider the nature of the cauſes of this lower price; it is always enough for him that it is ſo, and by the fact he muſt always be regulated. But although the nominal value of goods, in a ſociety in which freedom of commerce is allowed, muſt be regulated by the circumſtances already mentioned, yet between different ſocieties, there may be others. When we ſay that, in a certain ſociety, an article, bearing a given value, is juſt ſufficient to ſecure to the manufacturer all his expences, together with the ordinary profit, there is always a relation ſuppoſed between the ſum, repreſenting his expences, profits, &c. and the commodities, which that ſum is capable of commanding. We have ſeen, that the gold and ſilver imported into Europe from America, affected very conſiderably

the

the value of all goods and revenue. A manufacturer, would perhaps be better paid, in receiving two shillings, before the discovery of the American mines, than afterwards in receiving four, as the value of each portion of money was so much reduced, in consequence of the greater quantity. Thus, although we suppose that in every society the nominal value of goods is regulated by the quantity of labour and stock employed in their production; yet, the nominal value of goods, in general, may be different in different countries. A commodity, bearing a value of five shillings in Great Britain, may be sufficient to secure to the manufacturer his proper profits, &c. But in Portugal, a manufacturer employing the same quantity of stock and labour, (other things being equal) might require a sum of the value of six shillings, and yet, receive only his proper proportion of the revenue; that is, the value of money may be lower in Portugal than in England.

In addition to the commerce, arising from the advantages which one country enjoys over another, we therefore may discover the source of a more extensive connexion, in the differences which may take place, in the nominal value of goods in general, between different countries. It cannot admit of doubt, that if goods were considerably lowered in their value by any means in England, that it must prove of advantage to some individuals,

individuals, to carry a greater quantity to the markets of other countries; and as the quantity of gold and silver, which flowed into the different countries of Europe, raifed the nominal value of every fpecies of goods, fo any caufe which contributes to leffen the quantity of money in a country, muft on the other hand lower their value. If, therefore, a quantity of money be withdrawn from circulation, either by hoarding or otherwife, the nominal value of goods muft be affected; they muft confequently be carried out, and replaced by money. As the quantity neceffary for the circulation is introduced, if the caufe ceafe to operate, the nominal value of goods rifes to the fame level as the nominal value of goods in other countries. If money continue to be hoarded, there muft be an annual exportation of goods, fufficient to replace the quantity annually withdrawn from circulation. The demand, in this cafe, alfo, would be equal to the annual production, which would, however, be different in fpecies. The manufacturers who had employed their ftocks in the production of goods for which the demand had ceafed, (in confequence of certain people hoarding money, in place of putting it again into circulation, by the purchafe of goods,) would be obliged to turn their ftocks to the production of goods for the Spanifh or Portugal market. But as, in the cafes already mentioned,

tioned, they muft fuffer fome temporary loffes and inconveniences, until they had difpofed of the goods which at home had been rendered unfaleable. Thus the effects of hoarding, on the population and riches of the fociety, would be precifely the fame, as if the ftock and labour had been employed in the manufacturing of articles intended for confumption, without a view to reproduction. It can never be of the leaft confequence to fociety, whether its ftock and labour be employed in the production of articles of luxury, to be confumed at home, or in the production of articles to be fent abroad for the purchafe of gold and filver, to be buried. The application of ftock and labour is, in both cafes, unattended by any real advantage. The effects, however, of fuch a practice, would not be confined to the country in which it took place. The low price of the commodities carried to the countries, which had the command of the mines, coming into competition with their manufactures, muft reduce the profit in many employments. The demand for gold and filver being increafed, muft raife the profits of mining, which are at prefent (it is fuppofed) not higher than in other employments: many mines would be worked which now lie neglected, not being able to pay the expence of working. Thus, after things had gotten into a regular courfe, we fhould obferve a greater proportion

proportion of the stock of the country, in which the money was regularly laid up, employed in manufacturing articles for the purchase of the extraordinary quantity, and the quantity of stock driven out of employment in the other, in consequence of the extraordinary quantity of goods introduced, would be employed in supplying the demand for the unusual quantity of gold and silver. In both countries, there would be the same absolute demand and production as formerly, but different in kind.

From whatever causes a demand for gold and silver may arise, whether from their being a smaller quantity of them in one nation than in another, which by lowering the nominal value of goods, must induce individuals to carry money thither, for the purpose of purchasing them; or whether, although there be a large quantity, yet little remains in circulation, it must be the interest of individuals to supply that demand. Money must flow into such a country, as the other nations of Europe received it from Spain, after the discovery of the mines of America: for, although the Spanish government attempted to retain the exportation of it, by every means which ingenuity could devise; yet the interest which was found in carrying it to other nations, where the nominal value of commodities was lower, was so great, that to prevent it wholly was impossible:

ble: accordingly, it is fuppofed with a great degree of probability, that the deftruction of the Spanifh manufactures was in a great meafure occafioned, by the difcovery of America.

Thus, in whatever way we view the fubject, we fee the abfolute impoffibility, that, in the natural ftate of things, any part of the national capital, can remain for any confiderable time unemployed. Every interruption, however, in the ordinary courfe of the demand, muft neceffarily be attended by fome bad effects. To form, therefore, a right judgement of them, we muft take into view the fituation of focieties, with refpect to their connexions with each other; as, fhould we endeavour to draw our conclufions from the changes which take place in one only, they muft neceffarily be erroneous, as the affairs of commercial ftates are never indifferent to each other.

C H A P.

CHAP. XIII.

Money.

AFTER the division of employments has taken place, as the labours of each individual are employed on an article, of which in every cafe he confumes little, and in many none at all, the neceffity of fomething which may reprefent his labour, in order that he fhall, at the general market, exchange it for fomething of equal value, is manifeft. Money, therefore, is one of the links, which compofe the chain on which civilized fociety depends. As it was neceffary to fix on fomething which might be durable, and alfo, which could not be increafed at pleafure, the metals have generally performed this office, particularly gold and filver. We have feen, however, that the value of each portion, is by no means unalterable, but regulated by the quantity in circulation. The great quantity introduced into Europe, after the difcovery of America, confiderably reduced their value in the European market.

Authors have, in general, contented themfelves with the faƈt; but, in a work which profeffes an attempt to explain the principles of this fcience, it is neceffary to go farther, and if poffible, to get
a view

a view of the circumstances which so arbitrarily give a value to certain portions of them, at different times.

As the revenue of every individual is distributed and regulated in quantity by money, and as every portion of the real revenue, that is, the productions arising from the stock and labour of the society, is claimed by some person; it must necessarily follow, that there exists a relation between the nominal value of goods, or what is called their price, and the nominal value of the revenue of each; that is, when commodities are at a certain price, the labourer must receive a certain rate of wages, and the man of landed property a certain sum as rent. The profits of the owners of stock, are determined by a certain sum per cent. on its value. The nominal value of goods can therefore only regulate the nominal value of their stocks, and can have no influence in determining the number of pounds per cent.

In comparing the quantity of commodities, which any given quantity of money can command, at different times, we shall discover, that money, like other things, is changeable in value; at any particular moment, however, it is much less so than other things. It is less subject to decay, nor is the quantity brought to market, (or gold and silver which amounts to the same, as they may at pleasure be converted into money,) subject to
those

thofe fudden alterations, that many others things are. In conceiving the manner, therefore, in which its value is altered, we fhall be affifted, by fuppofing either a fudden increafe or diminution of it.

In the ordinary ftate of things, the nominal value of goods is always determined, by the quantity of money which appears for their purchafe. When the value of the rent of the landlord, and the other orders, as reprefented in money, remains ftationary, if the quantity of the productions, by any caufe, be either increafed or diminifhed, we always obferve a change in their nominal value. When the quantity of the annual production of corn, for example, is leffened or increafed, we always obferve a rife in its price, in the one cafe, and a fall in the other; that is, while the quantity of money remains the fame, if the quantity of the productions be leffened, the nominal value of goods muft rife. But we may reverfe the propofition, and it will be found equally true, that if the quantity of productions remain ftationary, and the quantity of money be increafed, that the nominal value of goods muft rife. If we were to conceive each individual to become fuddenly poffeffed of twice the ordinary quantity of money, while the quantity of the productions remained the fame, no one perfon could receive more than the quantity he had ordinarily procured, without

depriving

depriving some other person of a part of his proper proportion. But each endeavouring to procure as much as possible, it could have no other effect than to raise the nominal value of goods, just in proportion to the increase of the quantity of money.

Alterations in the nominal value of goods, under these circumstances, are absolutely necessary for the well being of society. If, when the quantity of the annual productions was lessened, the price were to remain the same, it must be attended by the worst possible effects. If, when the quantity of corn, for example, was smaller than ordinary, the price were to remain as usual; as the consumption of every order would remain the same, the quantity must be consumed before the return of harvest. Another good purpose answered by the rise of price, under these circumstances, is, that particular individuals do not suffer. If the farmer were to sell his corn at the ordinary rate, when his produce was small, he must suffer very considerably.

If we conceive, on the other hand, each individual suddenly deprived of half the quantity of money, which had usually represented his revenue, it must have the contrary effect. The demand might at first be for only half the usual quantity, but the farmer must sell his produce, as well to purchase articles for his immediate consumption,

consumption, as to continue his employment. The merchant and manufacturer, also, must dispose of their goods, in order to enable them to live: and pursue their ordinary occupations: but the farmer, in obtaining but half the usual price for his produce, can afford to give but half the usual rent to his landlord, and only half the usual wages to his labourers. The merchant, in selling his commodities for half the usual price, can afford to give but half the price to the manufacturer. The manufacturer gives but half the price to the farmer for raw materials, &c. and but half the ordinary wages to his workmen: but the landlord, on half the usual value of his rent, would procure the same quantity of consumable commodities, as formerly. The same with the workmen: merchants and manufacturers, for half the ordinary sum, would purchase the same articles, as well for their trade, as for their own consumption. Their profits would remain at the same sum per cent. as formerly, but their stocks would be represented by half the sum; 10 per cent. on £5000 would, in the one case, secure to them the same proportion of the real revenue, as on £10,000 in the other. Thus, in place of the man of landed property being worth £1000 per annum, he would be worth only £500. The labourer, who formerly had received two shillings

per

per diem, would now receive but one; and the stock of the merchant or manufacturer, which had formerly been reprefented by £10,000, would now be reprefented by £5000; but as the foil had remained equally fertile, and the workmen retained their fkill, the real revenue of each would ftill be precifely the fame.

As this part of our fubject is particularly interefting, and as we fhall have occafion to offer fome obfervations, which will require a pretty long difcuffion, we fhall divide the reft of this chapter into three parts.

PART I.

OF CIRCULATION.

We have feen, that the revenues of men in civilized fociety, are anticipated, and alfo, that the productions of certain places are confumed at the greateft diftances; and as the diftribution of revenue, and the commerce of every country, is performed by means of money: we are now to point out the quantity which may be neceffary for thefe purpofes, under different circumftances.

The

(97)

The more simple the state of society, the better shall we be able to trace the money through the different channels of circulation, and form a judgement of the manner in which its value is determined, and the quantity which may be necessary, while the value remains stationary. We shall suppose a society entirely confined within itself, but in which the division of employments is established. The owners of stock must necessarily be farmers and manufacturers; merchants and mercantile stock would be unknown and unnecessary. If we suppose that there are 52 people, including farmers and manufacturers, and each possessed of a quantity of consumable commodities, the value of £500 (exclusive of the value of their fixed stock,) the quantity of consumable commodities, in the society, will be of the value of £26,000. If it require just one year before the same quantity of goods can be produced, the annual revenue of such a society will be exactly £26,000. If wages of labour amount to one half of the produce, and they be paid weekly, a sum of £250 will be necessary. But as labourers do not always dispose of the whole amount of their wages, within the week, as they find it necessary to lay up a small sum, to provide themselves with cloaths, and for other expences, which must unavoidably clog, in a small degree, the wheels of circulation, a further sum will be necessary.

H   The

The expences of the owners of stock are also not perfectly regular; but if we suppose a sum in the society, of the value of their weekly consumption also, the whole sum in circulation will be £500. Whether more or less is of not the least importance, as we take this sum only for convenience. £500, then, will be sufficient to distribute an annual revenue of £26,000. If, in this state of things, a person were suddenly to appear with £500; in order to employ it with the greatest advantage, he must put it into circulation; but in purchasing materials from the farmer, he must come in competition with those who had formerly purchased them, which must raise their price. In hiring workmen, he must come in competition with their former employers, which must raise the rate of wages. In purchasing articles for his own consumption, he must also come into competition with those who had formerly consumed the whole of that kind of produce. Thus, in whatever way he employed his £500, it must affect the nominal value of every species of goods. All the goods, however, which he had procured, either directly for his own consumption, or indirectly, by giving to his workmen the command of a certain portion, must have been at the expence of those who had formerly consumed them. The farmer would sell his productions for twice the usual price, but for the money which
he

he had in his hands, he could procure but half the ufual quantity. The manufacturers, alfo, would fell their productions for double the ufual price, but for the money which they had on hands, they could procure but half the ufual quantity. As well, however, with them, as with the farmers, this could continue, only, till the additional £500 had got completely into circulation. When this had taken place, each owner of ſtock would fell his goods for twice the ordinary fum, he would alſo purchaſe the articles of his own confumption, at twice the old price. Wages of labour, alfo, would be increaſed in the fame proportion, and workmen would pay the advanced price in the purchafe of goods; but until this had happened, the owners of ſtock, and workmen, would loſe, in purchafing the articles of their confumption, and exactly what he gained; as the money was introduced, wages of labour, and the fum repreſenting the profits of ſtock would riſe, but the nominal value of goods would always rife before them, and the greater rife in the value of goods, than of theſe two ſpecies of revenue, would be juſt the loſs of the workmen and the owners of ſtock. The rife in the nominal value of wages, and the fum repreſenting profit, is the effect of the rife in the nominal value of goods, by the introduction of money. The loſs of theſe orders, and the gain of the owner of the additional

quantity

quantity of money, would depend on the quickness or flowness with which it was put into circulation. If the whole of it was put into circulation, within the term in which the quantity of money, already in circulation, was turned; that is, in a week, the nominal value of the goods for the confumption of that period, which had formerly been reprefented by £500, would, in confequence of the additional quantity of money poured in, be reprefented by £1000. In this cafe, however, the owner of the extraordinary quantity, would receive but one half of the goods; that is, what had borne before the value of £250 only. The workmen, in the mean time, would receive for their ordinary wages, but one half the ufual quantity of goods. The fame with the owners of ftock, fo that their lofs would be juft equal to what he had gained, £250. The next week, however, the owners of ftock could, with equal eafe, give double the common wages, and expend twice the ordinary fum of money; as every fpecies of goods would be raifed to twice the common price. If the money was introduced more flowly into circulation, the owner of it would derive ftill greater advantages, and confequently the other orders muft fuffer more. If he introduced but one half the firft week, or within the time in which the money, already in circulation, made one complete circumvolution, he would obtain, in the firft inftance,

one

one third of the goods at market; if, within the second period, he introduced the remainder, he would obtain a fourth of all the goods at market, making together seven twelfths of £500, in place of six twelfths, or £250. If put into circulation still more slowly, he must gain still more; but under every suppofition, the future effects must be the same, the rife of every species of revenue and of goods, in proportion to the quantity of money added to that in circulation. Thus the effect of the introduction of £500, under these circumstances, would be to raife the value of the stock circulating, or the confumable commodities sufficient for the ufe of the fociety, till those were produced, on which labour was employed, from £26,000 to £52,000, and the annual revenue alfo, in the fome proportion. If, in fuch a fociety, there was a neceffity for an accumulation of commodities for two years; or if, on an average, it required that length of time, before they could be produced; the quantity of money neceffary for the circulation, while it retained a certain value, would still remain the fame. The quantity of money, therefore, neceffary for the circulation of a country, while the value remains stationary, will depend on the quicknefs or flownefs with which it paffes, in diftributing the revenues of each individual, and not on either the amount of the annual revenue, or the quantity of stock.

But when commerce becomes more extended, when in every inſtance, two, three, or more people are interpoſed between the producer and the conſumer, the circulation becomes apparently more complex. The principles, however, which regulate the quantity of money, confiſtently with a certain value, remain the ſame. When the induſtry of particular towns or countries becomes employed in the production of but a few ſpecies of commodities, merchants and mercantile ſtock are neceſſary. Theſe are the connecting medium between different countries. In place of ſeeing the farmer go to the woollen manufacturer to purchaſe his cloths, or to the linen weaver to purchaſe his linen, he goes to the merchant. The money which the merchant receives, paſſes to the manufacturers in diſtant parts of the country, and thus the circulation is carried on in a more extenſive channel. When, alſo, lands are appropriated, and the owner receives his rent, in half yearly payments, the quantity of money, neceſſary for circulation, becomes greater. To this we are to add an additional ſum, neceſſary in thoſe countries that are heavily taxed, in which, according to the amount of the taxes, the money muſt be more or leſs interrupted in its channels. In every caſe, however, there is but a certain office to be performed by money, and if, while the quantity is ſufficient for the performance of this office, it be

increaſed

increafed, the value of the whole muft fall, or the value of goods and of revenue muft rife, in the proportion which the fuperabundant quantity bears to that quantity already in circulation. If employed in purchafing articles for immediate confumption, it muft come into competition with the money carried to market by the different orders, and which muft always be fufficient to command the whole of the goods at that time at market; or, in other words, thefe goods are the revenues of the different orders, and are diftributed to them by money. If this be increafed, it muft raife the value of each portion of goods, and each perfon muft receive lefs than ordinary. If employed in purchafing goods for fale, it muft come into competition with the money which had formerly enabled the merchants to procure the whole. In this cafe, alfo, it muft affect the nominal value of goods, in proportion to its quantity. In whatever way it is put into circulation, while the quantity of productions remains the fame, and while the money already in circulation paffes through the hands of the different orders, with the fame degree of velocity; it muft affect the nominal value of every fpecies of goods and of revenue. When money is introduced in this way into circulation, it affects firft the nominal value of goods, afterwards of revenue; after the whole quantity has got completely into circulation, the nominal value of

both,

both, (as we have already obferved,) is raifed in the fame proportion. If goods be doubled in value, revenue alfo will be doubled: but while the quantity of money in circulation, is increafing, every order of men fuffer in their revenues. It is in faƈt a tax, and will be more or lefs heavy, as the quantity is more or lefs great, and as it is put more or lefs flowly into circulation.

The increafe of money in a ftate, is by no means of the importance that is generally fuppofed. If one nation advances fafter than another in wealth and population, it will neceffarily acquire more money; but the acquifition of money is owing to the acquifition of real wealth, the increafe of the ftock and population, and a proportional increafe of the revenue. Were it poffible to prevent money from flowing in, that nation would advance ftill fafter in wealth and population. But while commerce exifts between nations, to prevent the importation or exportation of money, when individuals find an advantage in carrying it out of one country, or into another, muft be altogether impoffible. It is right, however, to give to each thing no more than its precife value.

Since the difcovery of America, we have feen the value of gold and filver gradually falling; we have feen, alfo, the revenue of the fovereign, which was derived from the mines, gradually become lefs, less. In the present day it is but trifling. The profits of stock, employed in working the mines, are also not greater than the profits in other employments. If the advantages and disadvantages of employing stock in the working, or searching of gold mines, be considered, it is generally supposed, that they are below the level of those in other employments. A man, it is said, who employs his stock in the search after a mine, is considered as almost irrecoverably lost; like one who would employ his stock in the purchase of lottery tickets, he may gain the prize, but the chances are against him.

For some time after the discovery of the American mines, their produce was so abundant, as to allow not only a considerable profit to the worker on his stock, but a very considerable revenue to the sovereign: but whatever we may suppose the fertility of these mines, if the quantity of the metals drawn from them, exceed the consumption, the revenues arising from them must gradually fall, until, at length, the whole of the produce be no more than sufficient to repay the owner of the stock, employed in working them, his expences together with his profits. The quantity which the sovereign receives, is added to the money already in circulation, as well as that which remains in the hands of the undertaker of the work. The value of each particular portion must, consequently,

quently, fall, as the quantity increases. No artifice, no tax can keep up its value. The revenues arising from these mines, have been, by a late celebrated writer, compared very unphilosophically, with the revenues arising from other mines. A tax on tin, or coal, or copper, may raise their value. If it amount to 25 per cent. what in one case would sell for £100, would in another sell for £125; but this is not the case with gold or silver. If it should amount to 25 per cent. on these, it could not raise their value in the smallest degree. The value of gold and silver is not determined as other things are, by the labour and stock necessary to procure them, together with the tax charged on them, but, whatever be the stock and labour necessary to procure a certain quantity, by the value of that already in circulation. If mines were discovered of a much greater degree of fertility, than those at present known, the value of the gold and silver obtained from them, would not be determined by the quantity of labour and stock necessary to procure them, but by the value of gold and silver already in circulation. If, on the other hand, the mines at present were to become less productive, or, if the quantity of stock and labour, in order to procure a certain quantity of these metals, must be increased, their value would not be determined by the additional expences and labour, but, as before

before by the value of thofe already in circulation. In this cafe, the miner muſt give over his employment, until the metals in circulation were raifed in their value, by a diminution of their quantity, by wearing, loſſes, &c. or until the quantity neceſſary for the circulation of the different countries became greater, in confequence of an increafe in wealth and population, which by enlarging the circle in which they pafs, muſt raife their value, unlefs the quantity be increafed; and thus, in the courfe of fome time, the employment might be refumed with the ordinary advantages. If gold and filver were withdrawn from circulation, and their place fupplied by tin or copper, the cafe would be reverfed. The value of the former might be raifed by a tax, while that of the latter would be determined by the quantity in circulation; the fame mode of reafoning is applicable in both cafes. A diſtinct view of the fubject may be thus given.

I. The gold and filver in circulation, in proportion to their quantity, regulate the nominal value of revenue and of goods.

II. If a quantity be added to that in circulation, it will lower the value of the whole, as the revenue which they diſtribute remains the fame.

III. The extraordinary profit of the worker of the mine, will be the difference between the quantity procured, and that neceſſary to repay

his

his expences, together with his profits, &c. The tax may amount to this difference of quantity.

IV. But, as the whole is thrown into circulation, as well the amount of the tax, as that sufficient to secure the undertaker of the work in the ordinary profits, &c. the value of the whole must fall, until the quantity drawn from the mine be no more than sufficient to reward the undertaker. When this takes place, in order that the profits may not fall below those in other employments, the annual production must not exceed the annual consumption, together with the additional quantity necessary for the circulation of improving countries.

Thus, we see the instability of that revenue which depends on gold and silver mines. The narrow policy of both Spain and Portugal contributed, however, to reduce it still lower. According to the old ideas, concerning political œconomy, it was supposed that the countries which contained most gold and silver, must necessarily be the richest. It seemed to be totally unknown or forgotten, that money is only the attendant on real riches, and that when these disappear, the other follows; without attending to this, every means were taken to prevent the money, obtained in South America, from passing into the other countries of Europe.

It must be evident, that had it been possible to have kept the whole of the gold and silver, in the countries to which it was first carried, the value of the money in circulation must have been much sooner affected, than had it been allowed to have been carried wherever the interest of individuals prompted them. The high value of that in circulation must, however, always determine the amount of the tax of the sovereign; but the attempt to keep it all within the country, must have directly tended to reduce its value. For, although the interest which individuals found in carrying it out in spite of every precaution, prevented the intention from being carried into effect; yet a part of the revenue which might be obtained from the mines, must nevertheless be destroyed, as the risk must always be equal to a certain proportion of the quantity thus procured. If, for example, in Great Britain a pound of gold represents a quantity of labour and stock as 15, while a pound of gold represents in Spain, in consequence of its greater quantity, a quantity of labour and stock as 11 only; if the exportation be allowed, a quantity will flow into Great Britain, until the value is nearer on a level; as it falls in value in Great Britain, it must rise in Spain, and just in the proportion which the quantity necessary for the circulation of Spain, bears to the

the quantity neceſſary for the circulation of Great Britain. The tax on the mine, may be increaſed in proportion to the alteration of value. But, if by penalties and puniſhments, the free exportation be prevented, the value of that in Spain muſt, at all times, be lower than that in England, by what may be ſuppoſed the riſk. If ſuddenly new means of preventing the exportation be diſcovered, they will for ſome time ſtop the exportation, until the quantity accumulated, (unleſs in conſequeuce of its reduced value, a ſmaller quantity be drawn from the mines) in Spain, by lowering the value of that in circulation, offers new temptations: like endeavouring by a dam to ſtop the courſe of a ſtream, it will at firſt have ſome effect, but gradually accumulating, it ſurmounts the obſtacles as they are ſucceſſively oppoſed to it, and can have no other effect, than to occaſion a difference of level.

The policy of Portugal has not been quite ſo abſurd as that of Spain, as the exportation of the metals was allowed on the payment of certain duties. As the opportunities of ſmuggling muſt, however, be more numerous than if the tax was levied at the mine; the revenue has always been lower than it ſhould have been. It appeared to be little underſtood in either countries, that the neceſſity of reducing the tax at the mines, was anticipated

ticipated by the prohibitions and duties at home. In both countries, alfo, the expence of maintaining certain officers, to enforce the execution of the laws relating to money, muft always have been confiderable.

PART II.

OF THE MANNER IN WHICH THE QUANTITY OF MONEY IN ONE SOCIEY AFFECTS THE QUANTITY IN OTHERS.

We have elfewhere mentioned, that the intereft which individuals may find in tranfporting goods from one country to another, muft depend on their nominal value. If, in two countries, the quantity of the metals in circulation be equal, in proportion to the offices which money has to perform, the commerce between fuch countries muft neceffarily be confined to the exchange of thofe articles, in the production of which each may have an advantage, either from nature or art; that is, to thofe commodities, which in confequence of lefs labour and ftock being neceffary to their production in one country than another, bear a lefs nominal value. If we fuppofe, however,

ever, the quantity of the metals in one fuddenly increafed, we fhall obferve a great alteration in the courfe of the trade, all nominal values muft be affected, many fpecies of goods, which had fold in both countries for nearly the fame fum, while the metals had remained of nearly the fame value in each, or whofe nominal value was not fufficiently low to allow of the expences of carriage, &c. muft be fo much affected in value, as to permit their importation with profit to certain people. Although we were to conceive two countries, whofe productions were precifely of the fame kind, whofe lands were equally fertile, and whofe workmen were equally fkilful; yet if, in one, the nominal value of goods, in general, be greater than the nominal value of goods in the other, and thefe countries to become known to each other, and a freedom of commerce eftablifhed, a quantity of the goods of the one, muft find a fale in the market of the other, and goods muft be carried in, and money out, until the nominal value of goods became nearly on a level. If a communication took place afterwards, it muft be owing to the introduction of improvements into both countries, but in the production of different fpecies of goods. Thus individuals, in each, would find an advantage in importing certain fpecies of goods only. The quantity regularly imported into the one, muft, however, always

ways be equal to the quantity exported, (if the two countries are advancing equally faſt in riches) as, were this not the caſe, the balance muſt be paid in money, which being added to that in circulation, muſt raiſe the value of that particular ſpecies of goods, on which the connection was founded, as well as others, and thus give encouragement to their being produced at home.

On the ſuppoſition we have ſtated, it may perhaps be worth while, to remark the real effects on each nation. According to the common ſuppoſition, it muſt be in favour of that which received the moſt money. The firſt thing we ſhould obſerve would be, a quantity of goods carried into the country which contained moſt money, which by coming into competition with thoſe at market, muſt lower the value of the whole. The quantity at firſt carried in, would not be ſufficient to reduce the value of the whole at market, as low as the goods in the other country; becauſe the intereſt of the perſon, who would carry the goods from the one to the other, muſt be regulated by the difference of value. The nominal value of goods in general muſt, however, be in ſome degree affected: we ſhould obſerve the labourer, on his common wages purchaſe a greater quantity of goods; the landlord alſo, on his ordinary rent, muſt procure a greater quantity; merchants and manufacturers, alſo, would be enabled to purchase the articles of their own consumption at a lower price; but they must be under the necessity of selling the articles of their trade, at a much lower also. But the merchant, in selling his goods at a lower rate, can afford to give a reduced price only. The manufacturer, in selling his goods at a lower rate, must reduce the wages of his workmen. The farmer, also, must be under the necessity of reducing the price of his produce, which must affect the rent of the landord: on every new importation of goods, the same effects must be produced, until at length, the great importation ceased, in consequence of the nominal value of goods in both countries being nearly on a level. When this had taken place, the rate of rent, of wages, and of goods, would be at the lowest. But while these changes were taking place, we should see the reduction of the value of goods, always going *before* the reduction of the nominal amount of each species of revenue. Every order of the state must gain: each species of revenue would be reduced; but the value of goods would be reduced in a still greater proportion. The nominal value of goods and of revenue, would be reduced, in consequence of the diminution of the money in circulation; the real revenue would be raised, in consequence of the increase in the quantity of goods. In the other country, effects of a

very

very different nature would take place; the first effect would be, the diminution of the quantity of goods, while the revenue, as reprefented in money, remained the fame: the nominal value of goods muft therefore rife*. By the introduction of

---

* In China, the value of money is higher than in Europe, and the Chinefe appear to be no ftrangers to this important fact in political œconomy. " With refect to commerce, the Chinefe entertain an opinion quite oppofite to that of every nation in Europe. Commerce, according to them, is ufeful, only fo far as it eafes them of their fuperfluities, and procures them neceffaries; on this account, they confider that, even, which they carry on at Canton, as prejudicial to the interefts of the empire. They take from us, fay they, our filks, teas, and porcelain: the price of all thefe articles is raifed through all the provinces, fuch a trade, therefore, cannot be beneficial. The money brought us by Europeans, and the high priced baubles which accompany it, are mere fuperfluities to fuch a ftate as ours. We have no occafion for more bullion than what may be neceffary to anfwer the exigencies of government, and to fupply the relative wants of individuals.

It was faid by Kouan-tfe, two thoufand years ago, that money, introduced by commerce, does not enrich a kingdom in any other refpect, than as it is introduced by commerce. No commerce can be advantageous long, but that which confifts in a mutual exchange of things neceffary or ufeful."—This will fufficiently fhew us, that this ingenious nation is well acquainted with the true principles of the political fcience. We fhall, however, give the reft of the paragraph, as it will be found to enforce many of the principles, we have attempted to eftablifh.—" That trade, continues Kouan-tfe, (whether carried on by barter or money) which has for its object, the importing of articles that tend to

of the money obtained in the other country, into circulation, each species of revenue would be raised in its nominal amount; but the rise of the price of the goods would always go before the rise in revenue. The real revenue would consequently be sunk, in consequence of the diminution of the quantity of commodities; the nominal revenue raised, in consequence of the introduction of money.

But although, such sudden changes can never take place; yet by taking a view of the state of nations at different times, with respect to the quantity of money in circulation, we shall be convinced, that changes have actually taken place, whose effects, although not very evident, from the slowness with which the money in cir-

---

the gratification of pride, luxury, or curiosity, always supposes the existence of luxury: but luxury, which is an abundance of superfluities among certain classes of people, supposes the want of necessaries among a great many others. The more horses the rich put to their carriages, the greater will be the number of those who go on foot; the larger and more magnificent their houses are, so much the more confined and wretched must those of the poor be; and the more their table is covered with a variety of dishes, the more must the number of those increase who are reduced to the necessity of feeding upon plain rice. Men, united by society in a large and populous kingdom, can employ their industry, talents, œconomy, and wisdom, to no better purpose than to provide necessaries for all, and to procure convenience to some."

See the Abbe Grosier's Description of China.

culation was increafed, are not the lefs real. Thofe lands, on which perpetual leafes were granted, whofe rents were referved in corn, yield a much greater fum to the proprietor, than thofe whofe rents were fixed at a certain nominal fum. The difference is by much too great to allow us to fuppofe, that it might be occafioned by the gradual increafe of rent (of which hereafter) or by different quantities of labour and ftock, being neceffary at different times, to produce the fame quantity of corn. We muft, therefore, fuppofe it owing to the increafed quantity of the money in circulation, and confequently the exportation of a quantity of goods. If the nominal value of commodities, in the other countries of Europe, had never been fo low, as to induce individuals to carry them to Spain; or rather, if the mines of South America had never been difcovered, which occafioned the rife of the nominal value of every fpecies of goods in Spain, the goods which had been fent out to purchafe the gold and filver, would have remained in the country, and the revenue of each individual, in proportion to his fhare, muft neceffarily have been greater. The revenue, therefore, drawn from the mines, was in fact a tax on the other nations of Europe; while the quantity of the metals increafed, the nominal value of goods and of revenue rofe, but the nominal value of goods always rose before that of revenue. The real revenue was reduced.

From what we have already said, it will be evident, that the quantity of money necessary to produce a very evident change, in the value of that in circulation, cannot be very great. If we suppose the money necessary for the circulation of a country, to amount to one fourth part of the annual income (whether more or less is of no consequence to our supposition) and this fourth part of 25 millions, it will require an addition of 25 millions only, to raise the revenue of such a country, from 100 to 200 millions. If mines were discovered which yielded twice the quantity of gold and silver, from the same labour and stock as those at present known, it would require a very considerable time, before they could produce their full effects; as all the nations of Europe, America, China, &c. would be affected nearly alike; and as the quantity drawn from the mines, could affect the value of that in circulation, only by the proportion which it might bear to it. The tax laid on the mines, might at first, be equal to one half of the produce; but as in this particular country, the quantity of money approached to 50 millions, the same increase taking place in others, the tax must be reduced, and when 50 millions were in circulation, the produce of the mine could afford none. But as we have formerly ly obfered, it would not require goods of the value of 25 millions, to purchafe this additional quantity; that is, goods which had borne a value of £25,000,000, before the difcovery of fuch mines. The firſt million introduced into circulation, would procure goods at nearly their former value, but the fecond would purchafe lefs than the firſt, and the third than the fecond, and as goods would be raifed to nearly double their value, when the 25th million was introduced, it could purchafe very little more than one half the quantity of goods that the firſt did. From the effects of the introduction of money into circulation, on the real revenues of the ſtate, we ſhall hereafter, have occafion to make fome important deductions.

PART III.

OF CIRCUMSTANCES WHICH MAY DETERMINE A GREATER QUANTITY OF MONEY TO CERTAIN SOCIETIES THAN TO OTHERS.

In the preceding parts of this chapter, we have ſhewn the manner, in which the quantity of money in certain focieties, regulates the quantity in others,

others, which may be fuppofed nearly on a level with it, in refpect to natural or acquired advantages. But where great differences in thefe take place, we fhall obferve great differences, alfo, in the quantity of money in circulation. We have already fhewn, that the nominal value which any commodity may bear, (confiftently with the quantity of money in circulation, which muft always be underftood) in order to fecure to the manufacturer his proper proportion of the revenue, or his profits muft be determined by the quantity of labour and ftock employed in its production, and the manner of the diftribution of the revenue. But in the production of certain commodities, it generally happens that a fmaller quantity of labour and ftock is neceffary in one place than in another. When this difference, which is always reprefented by the difference in the price, or nominal value, is fo great, as to allow of the expences of carriage, &c. from one country to another, the intereft of individuals induces them to carry them thither. It never happens, that in every fpecies of production, one country can have an advantage over another, almoft every country fupplies itfelf with the greater part of its food, and the coarfer manufactures; as, although there may be a difference in price at two places, it is feldom fo great as to allow the expences of carriage. But when we take all the

circumcumftance into view, which regulate the commerce between different nations, we fhall fee the abfolute impoffibility, that one nation can have fuch an advantage in the production of every fpecies of commodities, that it muft be for the intereft of individuals to carry goods out, and none into fuch a country. Let us fuppofe the inhabitants of a certain country to have fuddenly acquired the art of producing a much greater quantity of every fpecies of commodities, from a certain quantity of labour and ftock, than thofe in others; as the value of each article would neceffarily be lower than in other places, we fhould at firft, fee a quantity of every fpecies of goods carried out, and none in; but as thefe goods muft be paid for in money, the quantity added to that already in circulation, muft raife the nominal value of every fpecies of goods; their exportation muft be diminifhed, becaufe the intereft which the merchant finds in purchafing, muft always depend on the price at which he buys, and that at which he fells. It can never be of the leaft importance to him, whether a greater or lefs quantity of labour be neceffary to produce them, provided he can purchafe at a low price. If, however, in fpite of the rife of the nominal value of goods in general, there were fome which yet bore a lower price than thofe in other countries, they would continue to be carried out, and their value replaced by money.

money; but the still greater increase of the quantity of money in circulation, must be attended by a further rise in the nominal value of all goods. Thus the nominal value of certain kinds of goods must be so much raised, as to induce people to carry goods of the same kind thither from other countries, in which their nominal value was lower, in consequence of there being a smaller quantity of money in circulation, notwithstanding the difference of the quantity of labour and stock required to their production. The influx of such goods must lower the profits of those employed in producing those of the same kind, which would compel them to turn their stock and labour into some other channel, and notwithstanding the great superiority of skill and other advantages, the manufacture must be totally lost, and thus, in the course of some time, the quantity of the importation of goods would be just equal to the quantity exported, and the increase of the money in circulation, regulated by the same circumstances which regulate its increase in other societies. This furnishes us with another demonstrative proof, of the absurdity of that system founded on the ideas entertained concerning the balance of trade. We have already, in our chapter on the nature and manner of accumulation, shewn the absurdity of supposing the riches of a nation to consist in money, and here we have shewn the

limits

limits to its increafe, fuppofing a certain fociety to enjoy above others, every advantage of art and of nature.

In fuch a nation, however, although the nominal value of goods might be on the whole, on a level with thofe in other countries, notwithftanding the difference in the quantity of labour and ftock neceffary to produce each article; yet the real revenue of fuch a country muft much exceed that of others. Wages of labour, profits of ftock, and rent of land, muft be higher than in other countries*. In the increafe of the money in circulation, in countries on a level with refpect to particular advantages, we have obferved, that the merchants, manufacturers, &c. are fecured in their proper profits by the rife of the nominal value of their ftocks, while the number of pounds per cent. remain the fame; but in focieties which enjoy confiderable advantages over others, the fum per cent. is greater. Thus the natural rate of profit in one nation may be 10 per cent. while in another it may be as high as 12, or as low as 8 per cent. We muft not be underftood,

---

* An error into which all our writers on political œconomy have fallen, and which is the fource of many others, has been to fuppofe high wages or high profits, in general, the caufes of the high price of commodities, in place of confidering them as the effects of it.

to mean, that high or low profits mark the real state of the revenue of a country, for we shall have occasion hereafter to observe, that in some instances, while the real revenue rises, profit sinks; but, that in societies in other respects equal; that is, according to the actual state of their riches, the manner in which the revenue is consumed, whether with or without a view to reproduction, the revenue of one may be greater than that of another, and when this happens, the natural rate of profit must be higher. This natural rate of profit we shall have occasion to shew hereafter, to be more dependent on the produce of the land than the skill of the manufacturer.

CHAP. XIV.

Credit.

IN the mercantile world, we obferve a very extenfive commerce carried on without the affiftance of money, by means of credit: we perceive the merchant, by receiving credit, enabled to carry on a more extenfive trade, than if he were obliged to pay immediately for the goods in which he deals; the manufacturer, however, who gives it, muft be in a certain degree prevented from employing fo many workmen, as if he were paid immediately. It might, therefore, at firft fight appear, that it would be of advantage to fociety in general, and particularly to the lower orders, who are fo immediately dependent on manufacturing ftock, if credit were not allowed. But in looking to the true nature of commerce, or the exchange of commodities carried on between different countries, or different parts of the fame country, and of mercantile ftock, on which commerce between diftant places depends, we fhall difcover fuch a conclufion fallacious. The neceffity of a certain portion of mercantile ftock, we have already fhewn, and the proportion which it muft bear to the manufacturing in the different ftates of the fociety, society, consistently with the interest of each order. But if the merchant were obliged to pay the manufacturer for his goods, at the moment he received them, the quantity of mercantile stock, would be altogether insufficient for the business of the society. While credit is allowed, according to the length of time, a greater or smaller stock is sufficient to carry on a certain business. A man with a stock of £5000, with a certain credit, may be enabled to carry on as extensive a trade, as a man with a stock of £7000 or 8000 who receives none.

For example, if we suppose two towns, one of which furnishes the other with the woollen cloths of its consumption, which the other pays for in linens*, if to the merchants in each town, who dealt in those articles, credit had been given, and this credit suddenly withdrawn, we should see the woollen manufacturer enabled to produce a greater quantity of woollen cloths, and the linen weaver a greater quantity of linens; but a great part must remain unsold, as the merchant's stock must be insufficient, to enable him to supply the market, even with the quantity of its ordinary consumption, his profits must therefore be raised,

---

* Every place must ultimately pay for the commodities, which it receives from others, by its own productions; for though, in this instance, woollen cloths be paid for in money, yet linens must be sold, in order to obtain the means of purchasing.

while thofe of the manufacturer's were funk, which would induce the owners of manufacturing ftock, to turn it into mercantile, and thus the proper proportion would take place, in each employment. The quantity of ftock withdrawn from manufacturing, to be employed as mercantile, would be the difference between the quantity of ftock, which was neceffary in a certain manufacturing employment, while credit was allowed, and that, which would be found neceffary after credit had been abolifhed. The fame quantity of goods would be annually produced, the fame number of workmen employed; the only difference would be, that we fhould fay the mercantile ftock bore a greater proportion to the manufacturing, in the one cafe than the other. But even this affertion, though true in words, would be falfe in fact, becaufe, in common language, we call that manufacturing ftock, which is poffeffed by the manufacturer, and that mercantile, poffeffed by the merchant: but while credit is given, part of the ftock of the manufacturer is, in fact, employed as mercantile, which part of this ftock, after the abolition of credit, would be turned into mercantile, only by being poffeffed by a merchant, in place of its being employed by one. The nature of things would remain the precifely the fame.

In

In moſt employments, there is a certain credit eſtabliſhed, beyond which it cannot be carried, without injuring the manufacturer. When a perſon extends his credit beyond the ordinary time, he is ſaid to have traded beyond his ſtock. This, people of ſmall ſtocks, and of adventurous diſpoſitions, are often guilty of. It is always hurtful, as then the quantity of mercantile bears too great a proportion to the manufacturing ſtock.

This is the moſt ſimple form in which credit appears: it is ſometimes more complex. The manufacturer may give credit to a merchant, who gives credit on the ſame goods to a ſecond, and the ſecond again to a third; or the manufacturer may be paid for his goods by a merchant, who nevertheleſs may give credit on them to another perſon. All theſe, however, are to be reſolved into the general principle, that the ſtocks in the different employments, ſhall bear a certain proportion to each other, by which the buſineſs of the ſociety may be carried on with the greateſt poſſible advantage to all.

Thus, by credit, many very important advantages are obtained, if it were not allowed, the moment the ſtock in any employment became greater, than what could be employed with advantage, it would compel the owner to ſeek ſome other employment; but by credit the balance is

moſt

moſt nicely preſerved. If manufacturing ſtock increaſe in a greater proportion than the mercantile, by a long credit, the proper proportion may be preſerved. If mercantile ſtock increaſe faſter than manufacturing, a ſhorter credit reſtores the balance. To preſerve the proper proportions of ſtock in each employment, without credit, would be perhaps impoſſible, when we conſider the manner in which individuals make choice of profeſſions. It is impoſſible for any one to ſay, what profeſſion will be moſt advantageous, at a period not very diſtant, but the mere probability of this, and ſometimes even a whim founded on no probability, muſt determine every one. If the ſuppoſition be well founded, it often happens, that what may be a very profitable profeſſion one year, may be the reverſe the next, in conſequence of people turning too great a quantity of ſtock into it. Credit, in a great meaſure, provides a remedy for this evil, as by giving it, each individual may remain, and employ his ſtock, not certainly with ſo much advantage, as if he had employed it otherwiſe, but the difference may not be ſo great, as to induce him to change his employment, which muſt always be attended by very conſiderable inconveniences. It happens, alſo, that while the increaſe of ſtock in manufacturing employments, induces the manufacturers to give credit, it becomes the intereſt of the merchants to

K take

take it, and pay an advanced price on the goods, which is always in some degree regulated by the length of credit.

Credit, therefore, in the first place, serves, in some measure, to restore the balance between the parts of stock in the several employments. Its importance, however, in another point of view, is still more considerable: it enables both the internal and external business of the society, to be carried on by a much smaller quantity of money. Where it takes place, a very extensive commerce may be carried on between two places, without the necessity of any, or at most, of a very small sum of money passing from one to the other. For example, A is a manufacturer of cottons at Manchester, B is a merchant at the same place, C is a manufacturer of cloth at York, and D is a merchant there. If no credit were allowed, D would be obliged to carry money to Manchester for cottons, and B to carry money to York for cloths; but when credit is allowed, at the expiration of the time agreed on, A draws a bill on D, for which he receives money from B, who is indebted to C for cloths, D pays the amount of the bills to C, and thus, each person receives the value of his goods, without the necessity of money passing from one place to the other, except there be a balance, and even in this case, it is

often

often avoided by tranſactions a little more complex, but whoſe principles are the ſame.

The quantity of money which, without credit, would be neceſſary, is ſtill more evident, in taking into view the commerce carried on between diſtant countries. The quantity ſaved by credit, in a particular country, may not at firſt ſight appear great, as it is with ſo much eaſe carried from one extremity to the other; but acroſs the ſea, goods are as eaſily and as expeditiouſly conveyed as money; were we therefore to conceive Mancheſter and York ſeparated by a ſea, ſome thouſands of miles acroſs, and an extenſive commerce eſtabliſhed between them, if the manufacturers of each place refuſed to part with their goods until they received their value, the merchants could carry on little more than half the quantity of buſineſs, with the ſtocks which they employed while credit was allowed. A quantity of ſtock, muſt therefore be withdrawn from other employments, in order that the proportions, between the parts of ſtock in the ſeveral employments, ſhould be preſerved. The money which might be, on an average on the ſea, muſt be conſidered as totally withdrawn from the circulation of both places, and the ſtock withdrawn from the other employments, would be nearly equal to it: we ſay nearly, becauſe the quantity of ſtock, on the whole, muſt be diminiſhed, and conſequently there would

would no longer be a neceffity for the fame quantity of ftock in this employment. By enlarging the circle of circulation, the value of money is raifed, and goods are neceffarily fent abroad for the purchafe of the additional quantity. It is not, however, with a view to the public intereft, that credit is either given or taken. Manufacturers and merchants have an immediate intereft, in preventing money from lying unemployed, or being turned into unneceffary channels. It fhould rather indeed be faid, that the public is benefited through them.

But notwithftanding that the bufinefs of a commercial fociety may be carried on with lefs money, when credit is allowed, yet the quantity of money neceffary for circulation, always becomes greater, as the commerce of a country becomes more extenfive*. When a fociety provides itfelf with all the articles of its confumption, there is no neceffity for merchants or mercantile ftock; in this cafe, the money in circulation paffes from the hands of one member to the other without any confiderable interruption, and fometimes barter makes it unneceffary: but when, as in the

---

* It might however be fhewn, that the advantages arifing from this extended commerce, are neceffarily, at the very leaft, equivalent to the difadvantages, or additional expence, arifing from the neceffity of increafing the quantity of money in circulation.

more improved and rich countries, almoſt the whole of the productions paſſes through the hands of merchants, and as theſe productions are ſent in large quantities from one extremity of the country to the other, in order that they may better bear the expence of carriage, &c. the money in its paſſage is more affected; for in the inſtance we have juſt given, although there may be no neceſſity of money being ſent from York to Mancheſter, or from Mancheſter to York; yet, as there is a large quantity of goods to be paid for at a certain time, the merchant muſt prepare for it, by laying up a quantity of money, for which there would be no occaſion, if each place furniſhed itſelf with the articles of its own conſumption. The different operations of banking, the diſcounting bills of exchange, &c. provide however even for this, a remedy in many inſtances, which we ſhall ſhew more particularly at a future period.

The effects of all regulations, which tend either to increaſe or leſſen the quantity of the metals in circulation, while they retain the ſame value, or in other words, which clog or facilitate the paſſage of ſpecie, muſt neceſſarily be confined to thoſe countries in which they are adopted; for though they in one caſe receive goods, and in the other ſend goods, in exchange for money, to other countries, yet the real effects muſt always be felt at the mines: the money either thrown into or withdrawn from the circulation of other countries, in proportion to its quantity, muſt affect the value of the remainder, by which value the quantity of ſtock and labour, employed in procuring gold and ſilver, muſt always ultimately be regulated. If the value be raiſed, a greater quantity of ſtock and labour are employed, if leſſened, a part of that already employed, muſt be turned to the production of commodities for conſumption.

CHAP.

CHAP. XV.

Revenue.

IN the favage ſtate, the immediate produce of the labour of the individual, conſtitutes his ſole revenue. It muſt be abundant or otherwiſe, as nature is more or leſs kind in climate, and the ſpontaneous productions of the country. In this ſtate, although at all times equally vigilant, the rewards of his exertion muſt be ſubjected to unavoidable fluctuations. How widely different from this ſtate, is that of man in civilized ſociety: the produce of his labour may be ſubmitted to calculation, and even in thoſe countries leaſt favoured by nature, he enjoys conveniences, which man in an unimproved ſtate, though dwelling in the fineſt climate and moſt fertile ſoil, is altogether a ſtranger to. Nature, in the diſtribution of her favours, to the different countries of the earth, has been by no means impartial; in one, the labour of the huſbandman is rewarded by abundance, while in another, he with difficulty gleans a ſcanty ſubſiſtence. Civilization in part removes theſe differences, but it can never wholly do them away. Labour, employed on rich land, will always be more productive, than when employed on poor.

The greater or lefs fertility of the foil, is therefore, the firft circumftance which determines the revenue of the fociety. If one man be able to procure food for another, he may exchange half the produce of his labour for half that of the other; but if, in another place, one man be able to procure food for two more, and he exchange the food over and above that neceffary for himfelf, for the produce of the other two, value for value, determined by the labour employed by each, while in the one place, a man parts with half the produce of his labour for food, in the other, he parts with one third only. The conveniencies which each perfon enjoys, muft therefore be very different at each place.

But as the lands of civilized nations are appropriated, it may be faid, that the argument will not apply, and that the degree of the fertility can only regulate the rent of the land, and can have no fort of influence on the revenues arifing from wages of labour, or profits of ftock. If two tracts of land, unequal in fertility, lie near each other, the one will yield a much greater rent to the landlord than the other: the farmer, who rents the poor land, may find it as profitable as he who rents the rich, for as the produce is not fo great
in

in quantity, he muſt, in order to receive the uſual profits, give the value of a ſmaller quantity of it to the landlord: thus it may be ſaid, that the landlord receives all the advantages ariſing from the richneſs of the land, and that it can be of no conſequence to the reſt of ſociety, whether it be rich, or whether it be poor.

A concluſion of this kind, however, ariſes from a partial view. It is totally falſe, as a general principle; for this marks, only, the rent which one piece of land ſhall bear when compared with another, of a greater or leſs degree of fertility. It leaves us totally in the dark, with reſpect to the rent which land in general may bear. When we apply a thermometer to bodies of different temperatures, we can inform ourſelves of the relative degrees of heat, but we remain wholly ignorant of the abſolute quantity of heat contained in either. The manner in which the rent of land is regulated, will be conſidered in its proper place.

The ſecond circumſtance which determines the revenue of the ſociety, is the quantity of ſtock: unleſs it be ſufficient to allow of the diviſion of labour to its greateſt poſſible extent*, the revenue

---

* In the whole courſe of this work, we have conſidered the diviſion of labour in no other view, than as it tends to increaſe the quantity of the produce; in a moral view we have been totally ſilent on it, and it may indeed be doubted, if confining commerce

nue or produce arising from the united labours of the society, cannot be so great as it might be. The more simple the employment of the individual, the greater the produce must necessarily be on the whole; but the more simple the employments of each, the greater must be the quantity of stock. Society, in its unimproved state, is supplied with the necessaries and conveniencies of life, like a man who gleans subsistence from a barren soil, he is informed that at a considerable distance, every thing is produced in abundance, both to gratify his necessities and desires, a desert however intervenes, and before he can undertake the journey, he must collect provisions and cloathing, sufficient to last him till he arrives, Thus we see that, to accumulation, we are indebted for the numerous enjoyments we derive from the cultivation of the arts, and also for the power of displaying and exercising those mental powers, which in the pursuit of science, so eminently

---

commerce within narrow bounds, and consequently the division of labour which arises from it, would prove the best mode of correcting the moral depravity, so generally complained of, amongst the lower classes of men in civilized society, to which it is supposed, in a great measure, to give birth. A system of education comprehending the several classes, would certainly be more effectual, but to the support of which, a great revenue (which can only arise from freedom of commerce,) is absolutely necessary.

distinguish

distinguish man from the rest of the animal creation.

The third circumstance, regulating the revenue of the society, is skill in the arts; with respect to this, however, men are pretty much on a level, under the same circumstances.

From the productions of the soil and labour of the country, assisted by stock, arises every species of revenue, rent of land, wages of labour, and profits of stock, directly, and the revenues of the government which arise from these.

Every portion of the annual produce, is divided amongst the orders of which society is composed. Every increase of the revenue of the one, must, therefore, be attended by the diminution of that of another, while the quantity on the whole remains stationary.

The mark of a great revenue, is either the low nominal value of goods in general, and ffood in particular, (as we shall more particularly shew hereafter,) when compared with the nominal value of these commodities in other countries, or while the nominal value of goods in general, is on a level with those in other countries, a higher rate of rent of wages, and of profits of stock.

According as different species of revenue, rent of land, wages of labour, or profits of stock predominate, commodities (as we have already observed,) will be partially affected in their price, although

although commodities, taken in general, retain the same nominal value.

CHAP. XVI.

Of the Distribution of the Revenue.

FROM what has been already said, the manner in which the distribution of the revenue takes place, will be easily understood. The landlord is paid his rent, and the farmer his profits, by the produce of the land, bearing a certain nominal value, by which they obtain a certain proportion of the produce of the other orders in exchange. The wages of the labourer, or the consumable commodities which he can command, must, also, depend on the nominal amount of his wages. The profits of merchants, farmers, and manufacturers is the *residue*, and consequently must be either great or small, as a greater or smaller proportion is consumed by the other orders.

In a former chapter, we have observed that the rent of the landlord is anticipated by mercantile stock, although he does not receive it until some time after the farmer has had possession of the land; it is, however, still more directly anticipated, as much

much fo, as the revenues of the other orders. Manufacturers, merchants, and workmen, in difpofing of the money by which their revenues are reprefented, pay on the produce of the land, the advanced price which reprefents the rent of the landlord. At the moment, therefore, in which ftock anticipates their revenues, it anticipates, alfo, the rent of land. This is not immediately received by the landlord, as it has been found more convenient to pay it at certain ftated periods. Thefe anticipated revenues are repaid to the owners of ftock, by the produce of the whole of the labour of the country. This enters into their hands, in place of that which had been confumed. It muft, therefore, be evident, that their profits muft be the difference between that which they give, and that which they receive. Their proportion of the annual produce muft always be determined by the price of the produce of the land, and the wages of labour. The nominal value of all the commodities at market, muft depend on the quantity of money which appears for their purchafe. But if, while the quantity of money in circulation remains ftationary, the price of the produce of the land or wages of labour be raifed, the price of goods in general muft ftill remain the fame; it is altogether impoffible, that a rife in their value can compenfate for the rife of wages or produce: fome alterations

tions may take place, (as we have before obferved) in the price of particular articles, but as the quantity of commodities on the whole remains the fame, and as the quantity of money, alfo, is not increafed, the total value of all the goods at market muft be reprefented by precifely the fame nominal fum.

As in moft employments, the quantity of commodities produced, within a certain time, is liable to variations, it will be readily feen that the profits of ftock muft be affected. They are accordingly feldom for two years precifely the fame, but muft always be affected, as well by thefe variations in produce, as by the variations in the price of wages. It may alfo with propriety be faid, that the rent of land and wages of labour, although reprefented by the fame nominal fum, are at one time higher than another, in confequence of an extraordinary production, which muft ftill be reprefented by the fame quantity of money.

The confideration of the circumftances which determine, at different times, different proportions of the revenue to each order, will divide the remainder of this chapter into three parts.

PART

PART I.

RENT OF LAND.

In the sketch, which we now offer to the publick, it is not our intention to animadvert either on the manner, or justice, of the original appropriation of land, or on the nature of the tenure by which they are at present held, but to confine ourselves to pointing out the effects of *this mode* of appropriation on the several orders of society at this day.

Without tracing particularly the several steps of society towards improvement and civilization, we shall be sufficiently enabled to discover the extent and nature of these effects, by fixing our attention on that period of society immediately preceding the granting of land on leases, and from thence tracing the progress of rent.

The view of the landlord, in giving his land on lease, is to make more of it than if he held it in his own hands, that of the tenant in receiving it, to employ his stock as profitably on it, as if he were to engage it in some other employment.

The increased quantity of the produce, in consequence of the improvements and stock of the farmer, must be sufficient to secure to him not only

only the ordinary profits of stock, but to repay him for the expences of the improvements he may make during the term of his occupancy, on which the landlord at the expiration of the leafe demands an advance of rent. Unlefs the produce of the land bore a price, in the firſt place, fufficient to fecure to him the ordinary profits of ſtock; and in the fecond, to enable him to pay the rent of his landlord, it is fufficiently evident he muſt be a lofer. In order therefore to induce people to employ their ſtocks on the land, the price of the produce muſt be fufficient for both thefe purpofes.—What then, it is of the utmoſt importance to afk, are the circumſtances by which the price of the produce is regulated, which, in one country, is little more than fufficient to fecure to the cultivator the profits of ſtock, while in another it is alfo fufficient to allow a very confiderable rent to the landlord? Is rent regulated by the price, or is the price regulated by the rent?

The farmer in renting a certain quantity of land, muſt judge of what he can afford to pay by the quantity and price of the produce that may be raifed from it. It would appear, therefore, that the rent fettled on between the farmer and landlord was a matter perfectly indifferent to the reſt of fociety: if the farmer give too much, he only is injured by it, or if he give a lower rent than

than is commonly given, his profits are greater than ordinary, and it is of no importance to others. But this, however, apparently true with refpect to a particular farmer, is totally falfe when applied to all.

At the expiration of the term for which the leafe is granted, the landlord demands an advance of rent*. Although this advance be greater than the price of the produce enables the tennant to give, yet, as removing, the time before he can obtain another farm, and the want of employment for his ftock, are equivalent to a certain expence, he will generally be inclined to give it. Thus the rent of land is gradually encroaching, firft on the profits of the farmer, and fecondly on the revenues of the other orders: for as the produce of the land is of primary ne-

* Although there are fome landlords who do not rack-rent their tenants, yet they are like the lingering few in the rear of a flock, they ftill follow; for their tenants, without being injured, are enabled in a fhort time to advance their rents in confequence of the rife of price occafioned by the rife of rents in general, or the increafe in the quantity of produce by improvements, while the price remains ftationary. In a difcuffion of this kind, we muft give our attention to principles only, which, whether they influence the conduct of the individual or not, are always underftood. Thus, when we fay, a certain farmer has obtained h's leafe, on advantageous or difadvantageous terms, a certain eftablifhed rate of rent is underftood by the very terms we make ufe of.

L   ceffity,

cessity, the increase always depending on that of the stock employed, and as the profits of the farmer always depend on the price, so we see the necessity of a rise in the price, in order to enable the farmer to supply the market as plentifully as the demand requires; that is, to allow the increase of the stock on the land to keep pace with the increase of stock in other employments, and of population. This rise of price, unless in some degree counteracted by the introduction of improvements in agriculture, the necessities of the people will always compel them to pay.

While the rise of rent tends to raise the price of produce, these improvements tend to lower it; it would appear, however, that these improvements (for many have certainly been introduced) have not had so great an effect in keeping down the price, as the increase of rent in raising it. It would, we acknowledge, be unfair to judge by the present price of produce, as it is more than ordinarily high, in consequence of circumstances not regulated by general principles. We fancy, however, few will assert that the price of the produce of the land is, in general, lower now than formerly, or that improvements have not been introduced. Why then, should not the necessaries of life have fallen in price, in consequence of improvements, as manufactures fall on the same account? To this, we believe, no other answer can

can be given, than that the gradual encroachments which rent is conftantly making on the revenues of the induftrious members of the ftate, more than counterbalance the effects of all improvements.

As the cultivators of the land, in America, have little or no rent to pay, it is often fuppofed they fell their produce at a low price, becaufe they can *afford it*; but this is abfurd, for the price is low in America, not becaufe the farmers can *afford* to fell it at that price, but becaufe *they can get no more for it*; and the price is high in Great Britain, not becaufe the people think of the rent which the farmer pays, but becaufe they can get his produce at no other than a high price. When the price of articles in other employments is more than fufficient to allow the ordinary profits of ftock, it provides of it itfelf a remedy for the evil. Stock, in confequence of thefe high profits, is more rapidly accumulated, the market more plentifully fupplied, and the price at length no more than fufficient to allow the common profits: but the high price of the produce of the land provides no fuch remedy, as the whole, above that abfolutely neceffary to leave with the farmer the ordinary profits, enters the pocket of the landlord, and in place of returning to the land, fo as to increafe the produce, is diffipated. It is becaufe almoft the whole above that neceffary to maintain the farmer returns to the land in America, (we fay almoft the whole, for even in America the lands in fome of the ftates, are not fufficiently divided) that the price is low, and becaufe the reverfe takes place in Britain, that the price is high. Let for a moment be conceived the ftate of Great Britain, if twelve millions, the fuppofed amount of rent, were annually returned to the land, fo as to increafe its produce; where would there be a demand for fo immenfe a quantity? and what would be the effects? Let not exportation be fpoken of, for thefe principles are as applicable to other countries, as to Great Britain.—We muft be convinced that a very confiderable fall in the price would be the confequence, and that in a fhort time, it would be no more than fufficient to allow the farmers to fupply the ordinary demand of the market. Profits, as well in the farming as in other employments, and wages, muft in confequence of the reduced price be raifed; for the price which the produce at prefent bears, equally affects profit in all employments and wages.

When profits of ftock and wages of labour are higher in one country than in another, if the advantages of both are equal, it can arife from no other circumftance, than that, in one the idle and worthlefs confume a greater proportion of the annual

nual produce than in the other. In America, both wages of labour and profits of stock are higher than in Great Britain, yet America labours under many difadvantages, compared with Great Britain, her lands are not fo well cultivated, nor have thofe great divifions of labour taken place, which the more abundant stock of Great Britain allows, and by which her revenues are confiderably augmented. But in the former, the induftrious enjoy almoft the whole of the produce of their labours, while in the latter, they are oppreffed by the law of entail and enormous annual taxes. The fyftem from which the latter have arifen, we fhall hereafter fhew to be in the higheft degree unjuft and impolitic.

The evil effects of the law of entail, are, however, to be traced yet further; for, exclufive of depriving the people of fo large a portion of their revenues, by preventing every kind of expenfive improvement, it prevents thofe revenues from being fo great as they otherwife would be. All improvements ceafe for fome years before the expiration of the leafe, which is fcarcely ever long enough to allow of expenfive ones with any advantage.

Superior fertility, improvement, or fituation, are the only circumftances which ought, or, were the lands divided, would give, to the owners of certain portions, a greater fhare of the annual produce than they were entitled to from their labours.

We have already shewn, that an increase of population can never go before an increase in the quantity of those goods which are distributed to the lower orders as wages. When wages are high, it is a demonstrative proof that an increase of these commodities has taken place, and that the labour and stock of the society had been employed in agriculture and the useful manufactures, in place of providing articles of luxury for the consumption of a few. There are but two ways in which stock and labour can be employed, either in providing the means of subsistence for a rising generation, or in administering to the vices of a few. This we have already noticed, but we hope its importance will apologize sufficiently for the repetition.

Such a division of property*, as would naturally

---

* The Chinese at a very early period appear to have been well aware of the beneficial effects of a division of the lands, as,

" Hoang-ti III. Emperor of China, according to the Chinese accounts, measured the country and divided it into Tcheou; he made several principalities of 100 Lys each, where he built towns; he ordered that 240 paces in length and one in length should make a Mou; that 100 Mou should make a King; so that the pace being 5 feet, a Mou of land contained 6000 square feet, and 600,000 a King. He also ordained that King should be called Tsing,

that

rally take place, by the abolition of all laws, which tend to keep it in the hands of a few, can alone compel every individual of the ſtate to be uſeful to it, and determine ſtock and labour to thoſe employments, in which they muſt neceſſarily be engaged, in order that the ſociety ſhall advance in population and wealth, and that the claſs of people, by which all are provided, ſhall enjoy, at leaſt, a reaſonable ſhare of the produce of their own labours.

PART II.

WAGES OF LABOUR

From what we have had occaſion to ſay, in the preceding parts of this work, the variations which take place in the ordinary rate of wages, will be ſufficiently underſtood; little remains therefore in this place for us, but to give an abſtract of them.

Before the accumulation of ſtock, and the introduction of the arts, the rewards of labour, as

that it ſhould be the portion of eight families, which ſhould have each a King or a 100 Mou, and the remaining in the middle, ſhould belong to the Emperor, and be cultivated at the common expence of the eight families." Du HALDE.

we have already obferved, muft depend on the fpontaneous productions of the foil, nor could the number of inhabitants ever exceed what they could maintain. But when, by the accumulation of riches and their employment, the means of fubfiftence is increafed, we difcover the dependence of the labourer on their owner. As, with the affiftance of ftock, a much greater quantity of goods may be produced, than by labour merely manual, thofe poffeffed of it, had it always in their power to procure labourers fufficient to put it in motion. Workmen, for wages equal to what they made of their ufual employment, or a very little more, would engage themfelves to an employer. Wages of labour, therefore, would not at firft be regulated by what the owner of ftock could afford to give, but by what thofe made who were not employed by ftock. But as ftock increafed, and became fufficient to employ the whole of the labour of the country, a new order of things followed. Millions then became dependent on that ftock, by which they were employed and fubfifted. It proved as it were a new foil. The advances of moft of the nations of the world, have been fo flow, that it is only by abftracting our ideas a little, that we can be enabled to judge exactly of what has taken place. We muft annihilate time, (if we are allowed the expreffion)

preffion) and bring the ftate of a nation at different periods, at once under our view.

In the various degrees of the quantity and increafe of this accumulation, we are, therefore, to look for our ftandard of wages. After the ftock of the country has become fufficient to give employment to the whole of the labourers, their wages muft neceffarily be determined by its increafe. We have already fhewn, that in the advances of a ftate in wealth, ftock is not employed where it accumulates; that as the market for the productions of a country, becomes more extended, a greater proportion of the national capital, is employed by the merchant. The effects of this on the revenues of a country, by allowing and fupporting greater divifions of labour, we have already fhewn. It occafions, however, wages of labour to advance more flowly, but as it allows the ftock of the country to be more rapidly accumulated, and as ftock approaches to that ftate, which admits of the greateft divifions of labour, and confequently of the greateft poffible revenue, wages of labour rife much higher, than if freedom of commerce was not allowed. In every cafe, an increafe of ftock is attended by the rife of wages, and any thing which tends to prevent its accumulation, (unlefs by confining commerce within certain bounds, by which labourers enjoy a temporary advantage,) muft keep down the rate

of

of wages. Want of œconomy in the owners of ſtock, who are however ſufficiently inclined to it, unleſs overpowered by example, and other inducements, is the firſt circumſtance which reduces the rate of wages; the diſſipation of a large portion of the annual revenue, by the law of entail, the ſecond; the diſſipation of a ſtill larger portion, (as we ſhall hereafter more particularly ſhew,) by annual taxes, the third; and improper reſtrictions on commerce, the fourth. Labourers ſuffer by theſe, in common with the other members of the ſtate.

As, in a thriving country, the principal expence of the lower orders, is in food, ſo its price will have conſiderable effect on the rate of wages. When the price of food is low, although the rate of wages may be ſomewhat lower on that account, the real rewards of labour are more conſiderable. When the price of food is raiſed, although attended by a riſe of wages, yet the riſe of the latter, can never compenſate for the riſe of the former; as, in conſequence of the greater wages, the owners of ſtock muſt in ſome degree be prevented from accumulating. The riſe in the price of food, affects both the wages of labour and the profits of ſtock.

PART

PART III.

PROFITS OF STOCK.

It will fuffice to give a fhort abſtract of the variations in thefe, alfo, as they muſt be fufficiently underſtood, from what we have faid in the courfe of the work. Independently of the variations to which the profits of ſtock are liable, in common with wages of labour, as the ſtate of the fertility and diviſion of the lands, and the ſtate of the arts with refpect to improvement, they are altered by circumſtances peculiar to themfelves. As the accumulation of ſtock approaches to that ſtate, which admits of the greateſt poſſible diviſions of labour, and confequently the greateſt production; and when an increafe of people muſt attend every further increafe of ſtock, the quantity of the annual productions, diſtributed as wages, by degrees, bear a greater, and that diſtributed as profits of ſtock, a lefs proportion to the quantity produced on the whole; confiſtently, however, with another circumſtance, the degree of the œconomy of the owners of ſtock, when they confume the whole of their profits, wages of labour can never be greater, than to allow the race to be kept up, whatever be the ſtate of accumulation, or the

annual

annual produce. In China, it would appear, that the owners of stock consumed annually the whole of the amount of their profits, as they are there remarkably high, and wages, it is said, remarkably low; the interest of money, which always marks the state of profit, being according to most authors, as high as 30 per cent*.

* It may not, perhaps, be unnecessary to remark the mistake into which Dr. Smith has fallen, with respect to the effect of a great population on wages, and a great accumulation of riches, on profits of stock. Although one should be accompanied by the other, the competition, which would naturally arise, he is of opinion, must reduce the rate of both wages and profits. The doctor seems not to have known, that competition never annihilates, but on the contrary serves, in two ways, to increase rather than to diminish the annual produce, and consequently the different species of revenue; first, by laying every individual under the necessity of exerting himself; secondly, by preventing a greater quantity of stock, from being engaged in any employment, than what at a certain time may be necessary, and which, (as we have elsewhere observed,) is only relative to the quantity of the whole. Competition, in reducing wages and profit, reduces, he supposes, the price of goods, (in conformity to his theory, on the manner in which the nominal value of goods is regulated, which we have endeavoured to shew is unfounded) but the public he is, of opinion, must gain by this reduction. It would certainly be not a little difficult to prove, that the public can gain, while the individuals, composing the public, lose. The doctor cannot be supposed to mean, that it is of advantage to the public, to reduce the quantity of goods, produced within the society, in proportion to the people amongst whom it is to be divided: and this alone can be understood; for if these goods are produced, they must be divided, and this division must necessarily be made by a certain

rate

rate of wages, profit, rent, &c. In China, certainly the richeſt and moſt populous country in the world, the intereſt of money, (which marks the rate of profit,) is conſiderably higher than in any part of Europe. The doctor, in accounting for this fact, ſo directly contrary to his theory, is obliged to adopt a ſuppoſition, the truth of which is extremely doubtful, and though true, altogether inſufficient to account for it. The high rate of intereſt in China, and the low rate in Europe, we believe, may be very ſatisfactorily explained, on the principles we have endeavoured to eſtabliſh. In the former, the great accumulation of ſtock, and a free internal trade, at leaſt equal to that of all Europe, allows and ſupports thoſe very great diviſions of labour and ſtock, by which the annual productions, in proportion to the numbers amongſt whom they are to be divided, are conſiderably increaſed. In the latter, a ſyſtem (of which it would be unbecoming a philoſophical enquiry, to ſpeak in the terms it deſerves,) gives birth to commercial reſtrictions, by teaching the people of one part, to conſider thoſe of another, as their natural enemies, and conſequently prevents many diviſions from taking place, which their ſtock (ſcanty compared with that of China,) would otherwiſe allow. The law of entail alſo takes place, which throws a conſiderable portion of the annual produce into the hands of the idle, and a ſyſtem of taxation, which acts as commercial reſtrictions, in reducing the annual produce, and as the law of entail, in ſupporting the idle with the produce of the induſtrious,

CHAP. XVII.

Taxes.

AGREEABLY to our general plan, we shall treat of the more general effects only of taxes. On this part of our subject, we confine ourselves the more willingly, as we shall hereafter have occasion to place the nature of taxes in general, in a point of view, which will make a particular discussion of them unneccessary.

We should define taxation, to be for the purpose of giving to some members of the state, a part of the annual produce of the labour and stock, in the production of which they had not assisted. Concerning the effects of the taking from one citizen to give to another, many ingenious men have employed their pens. Those who were of opinion that it was hurtful, were not able to shew the precise manner in which it acted. Accordingly, the other party appears to have been most numerous. The argument on which they found their opinion, is, that as the annual production is not diminished by taxes, and as their amount is spent within the country, they cannot be injurious to it. In what view then are we to consider this expression; " not injurious to the country?"

country?" Are we to suppose, that its advances in wealth and population are not impeded by taxes, or the exertions against an external enemy not enfeebled? These appear to us, to comprehend the principal modes in which such an assertion can be taken. When carefully examined, however, both propositions will be found unsupported.

In the first place, the power which the merchant or manufacturer has of accumulating, must depend on his profit; any thing which reduces the one must affect the other. The power of the workman to support a family, must depend on the rate of his wages, and the quantity of consumable commodities which he can procure for them. A tax, raised on the commodities of the ordinary consumption of the merchant, the manufacturer, or farmer, must increase his expences, his ability to accumulate must consequently be impaired; but as the wages of labour must depend on the increase of stock, they must be reduced. Thus taxes, on the expences of the owners of stock, fall in part on the lower orders of people. If taxes, on the other hand, be laid either directly on the wages of labour, or on the commodities of the labourers' consumption, wages of labour must be raised, and thus affect the profits of stock. Taxes, therefore, on the commodities consumed by the owners of stock, or the labouring part of

the

the community, according as they are more or less heavy, directly prevent the advance of a society in wealth and population.

But it may be said, that taxes imposed on the articles of the luxury of these orders, particularly on those of the lower order, are rather serviceable, by preventing the poor from disposing of so much of their money, in the purchase of these articles, and thereby enabling them to supply their families more plentifully, with the articles of immediate necessity. But we would ask, what would take place if the poor were wholly to discontinue the use of such commodities? Taxes must still be raised, and when found not productive in one way, must be laid on in some other; and if they can be found productive on no other commodities, than those absolutely necessary to life, they will be laid on them. Let us suppose, for a moment, a nation in this state. The man with the largest family, and who is generally the most industrious, must be the greatest sufferer. Marriage must, therefore, necessarily be discouraged: the society which men had, in one state, sought for in their familes, would in the other, be found in the porter house; and, as taxes were found unproductive or ruinous, when imposed on the necessaries of life, they would in the course of a short time, be laid on those articles, (malt and spirituous liquors, for example,) the demand

for

for which had been increafed, probably on account of the neceffity of thefe taxes. To lay taxes on thefe articles, and, at the fame time, to accufe the people of being addicted to debauchery, which is in fact done by their being held forth as fo very productive, is (to ufe a very vulgar expreffion,) to knock a man down and kick him for falling. We fhould not confider taxes, as being of no differvice, becaufe laid on fuch articles, but as ruinous, in being the fountain head of debauchery. Were there no neceffity for thefe enormous taxes, was each man left in poffeffion of the whole of the produce of his labour, the manners of men would no longer be the fame. It is remarked, that thofe who emigrate to America, and who are generally the dregs of our ftreets, in a fhort time totally change their manners; after their landing, from the cheapnefs of liquor, they wallow in drunkennefs and filth; but want of companions, and the tacit reproach of thofe of their own rank, in a different conduct, work by degrees a change, and after they have forgotten the villainous tricks, nurfed by the vices of Europe, become ufeful members of fociety.

·But, although the debauchery of the lower orders, be fuppofed to arife from fome other fource, and though we were to fuppofe their confumption of thefe articles, to be the fame, whether there may or not be a neceffity for thefe taxes; yet, in the point of view, in which it more immediately belongs to our subject, to consider the effects of taxes, they are still the same; that is, they directly prevent the accumulation of stock, and the advance of the society in population. Those who first peopled America, carried with them all the ideas of Englishmen, and pursued nearly the same mode of management, and yet, we observe the one nearly stationary, and in the other, the population doubled within the term of twenty years, and their wealth much more than doubled within the same period. This great difference some have attempted to account for, by the vast extent of land*, of which the Americans have the command, but land uncultivated can produce nothing; and that which is under cultivation, produces in proportion to its extent, and the labour bestowed on it, a much smaller produce than the lands of Great Britain. But in the former, the

---

* If we reflect a moment, this will appear altogether insufficient to account for it. For on an average, perhaps not more than one third of the whole continent of Europe is cultivated, and that which is under cultivation, could be made to yield a much greater quantity of produce. In Great Britain and France, two of the most improved countries of Europe, there are yet immense tracts of waste land: in the former, according to a late account, 18 millions of acres; in the latter*, 40 millions, a great part of which is absolutely waste, and the rest almost useless, from the miserable manner of cultivation.

* See Young's Travels.

industrious

induſtrious enjoy the whole produce of their labour; in the latter, 12 millions are annually diſſipated by the law of entail, and 20 by the annual taxes. Let any one conſider what would take place in Great Britain, if 32 millions were annually divided, ſo that one part ſhould go to the labourer, and enable him to raiſe a more numerous family, and the other to the augmentation of the profits of ſtock, to enable the quantity to keep pace with the population, and the ſtock to go on accumulating in the ſame proportion, like compound intereſt on a certain ſum, attended by a proportional increaſe of the population.

With reſpect to the ſecond effect of taxes, on the power of a ſtate. This muſt, on even a ſuperficial view, appear abundantly plain. The power of every nation muſt depend on the numbers it can maintain in the field, and the other expences attendant on war. But this power directly depends on what each individual can ſpare from his ordinary conſumption; or, in other words, what he can afford to pay as taxes. Every tax, therefore, by leaving to each individual a ſmaller portion of the produce of his induſtry, muſt directly weaken the power of every ſtate. If the whole amount of the Engliſh taxes were employed in carrying on the war, in place of part being appropriated to the payment of the intereſt of her debts, can any one doubt of her being more powerful.

Another general effect of taxes, is, not only to diminish the revenues of the individuals of a state, but to prevent these revenues from becoming so great as they otherwise would. This must depend, chiefly, on the mode of levying them. In no country of the world, perhaps, are such enormous taxes raised, as in Great Britain, without injuring the subject further than the taxes themselves; or in no country are they raised in so unexceptionable a way. They must always be hurtful, and when carried to a certain length, ruinous; but in many countries, the mode of levying them, is perhaps much more ruinous than their amount. The Alcavala of Spain, is observed by authors, amongst whom is the judicious Dr. Smith, to be of this kind. Common sense, and our best authors, agree in pointing out the almost perfect freedom of commerce, as the cause of their being comparatively less ruinous in Great Britain, than in other countries. But as every species of tax must more or less prevent the freedom of commerce, it must necessarily have some effect on the revenues of a nation. In many cases, a second tax arises from the first which is imposed by government. The tobacco merchant, for example, must have a stock sufficient to pay not only the value of the tobacco, but also the duties imposed by government; in disposing of the tobacco, he must therefore charge not only an advanced price, in consequence of the

the duty, but alfo a profit on the part of his flock advanced to pay it: an increafe of expence takes place in this way pretty generally.

But taxes are not confined in their effects, to the diminution only of the revenues of the members of the ftate, or to impeding the future progrefs of a nation in wealth; they may, when carried to a certain height, directly affect the capital ftock. When taxes, together with the ordinary confumption of the people, exceed the annual revenue of the fociety, the ftock muft be encroached on; and as taxes, in confequence of it, muft become from year to year lefs productive, there follows the neceffity of heavier impofitions on what remains; and thus affairs become more defperate; bankruptcies, and the poor thrown out of employment, (unlefs arifing from an alteration in the courfe of the demand,) are an infallible n ⁀ of it. A nation may, however, hold out fo⁀ ny years, under the preffure of a load une⁀ to its ftrength. The merchant ftill buys and fells, the manufacturer ftill employs workme⁀, but their profits are not equal to their confumption; their ftock always returns to them of lefs value than when fent out, and muft in the end wholly difappear.

Thus, in focieties where the natural order of things takes place, taxes are deftructive to both the individual and the community. But in thofe where

where the law of entail takes place, a tax may be raifed on the

RENT of LAND.

We have already fhewn the nature of this fpecies of revenue, and the circumftances by which it is regulated. A tax, therefore, laid on it, does not affect the other orders of fociety.

In many cafes, taxes may be partially impofed, with great advantage, on articles of luxury. As the tax on fpirituous and malt liquors. For when we fay debauchery is encouraged by taxation, we fpeak of it only as a general effect of taxes. When taxes are impofed on articles of luxury, they muft fall lefs heavily on the induftrious poor, than when impofed indifcriminately, or on the articles of immediate neceffity. The inducements alfo to marry, and attach themfelves to their families, muft be felt more ftrongly by the lower orders. In ftates, however heavily taxed, the lower orders muft either be very miferable or debauched. When young men, in place of marrying, lead a diffolute life, and fpend the money in hurtful gratifications, which would enable them to rear up a family, they really afford effential fervice to that part of the lower order, which is directed by a different conduct. The wages of labour are neceffarily kept up, by which the induftrious, who rear up families, are much better fupplied supplied. If, in states heavily taxed, the lower orders were to give up the custom of unnecessary indulgence, and appropriate the whole of their wages to the maintenance of a family, the number of people must increase considerably faster; but as their numbers cannot long run before stock, wages of labour must fall, and the profits of stock rise; that is, the whole of that unnecessarily consumed by the lower orders, would be divided, so as that one part should go to maintain a greater number of people, and the other to the augmentation of the stock. The population and riches of the country would increase somewhat faster, but the conveniences and necessaries, which each individual could command for his family, must be much less. Thus it is necessary, that one half of the workmen should be debauched and live single, in order that the other may be enabled to live tolerably, and raise up families, so that the numbers of people may be kept up. Corrupt manners act like taxes, by impeding the progress of society in wealth, and when carried to a certain length, with taxation, assist in its downfall.

In the imposition of taxes, a rule which should never be departed from, is, to lay them in such a manner, that the payment of them cannot be eluded without serving society. All taxes on articles of luxury, are laid agreeably to this rule; all taxes on articles of immediate necessity, and

particularly

particulary on the neceffaries of life, are laid in oppofition to it. The former, incline the people to induftry and good morals; the latter, to idlenefs and profligacy. If every perfon, in proportion to his ability, really wifhed to contribute his fhare to the public expence, it would be matter of no importance where taxes were laid; if on the neceffaries of life, and young men continued to marry as ufual, they would not prove more pernicious than when laid on other things, becaufe, wages of labour would rife in a certain proportion: but from the ignorance of fome, and the felfifh motives of others, it is neceffary to put men into the right path, by various methods.

A fpecies of tax in oppofition to the rule we have mentioned, is the

TITHE.

The effects of the tithe has been much contefted; what we have to fay on it, may be given in a very few words. It is neceffary in the firft place, to remark, that it is impoffible to form a true judgement of its effects, from partial inftances. When certain lands are free from the tithe, the owner enjoys all the advantages; when the farmer can elude the payment, he is gainer; but it would be abfurd to infer from thence, that if all lands were free from the tithe, the landholders alone would gain; or if all the farmers could eafily elude

the

the payment, that they would be benefited by its whole amount. We have shewn the circumstances on which the state of rent depends, and that the revenue of the farmer is regulated by the price of the produce of the land, which cannot, as in other employments, be for any confiderable time, greater than to secure to him the ordinary profits. If the tithe were abolished, it must be evident, that the farmer could afford to sell his produce at a price lower than common, by its whole amount, after paying the usual rent to his landlord. If he did not make the reduction immediately, competition and the greater increase of stock on the land, than in other employments, must in a short time compel him. Landlords, farmers, merchants, and manufacturers would equally gain by the reduction in the price of food, but particularly the industrious poor, whose expences are chiefly confined to it.

Much more could be said on the hurtful effects of the tithe, which from their being already well known, we think it unnecessary to repeat.

CHAP.

CHAP. XVIII.

National Expences.

THESE are, either the ordinary annual expences, necessary for the support of the state, or the extraordinary ones in which a nation may be involved, in consequence of wars, &c. The amount of the former, is generally paid by annual taxes; the latter may be advanced by individuals, who receive a certain sum per annum on the amount. Thus, in most of the nations of Europe, the sum necessary to pay the interest of the debts, makes a very considerable, and often the greatest part of the annual taxes. The system of borrowing, in place of laying a tax equal to the amount of the extraordinary expences, has been approved, on the supposition, that it was much less destructive: as it was supposed that, in the one case, a man parted with but a part of his income, while in the other it must diminish his stock, and consequently reduce the stock of the country, the whole amount of the extraordinary expence. To discover the truth of this proposition, it will be necessary to know in what manner the stock and revenue is affected
under

under each fuppofition. In the firft place, the ftock which is lent to government is confumed without a poffibility of reproduction. It is taken directly from one or other of the three divifions of ftock ; if from the mercantile, part of the other two branches of ftock muft be turned into the channel from which fo much ftock had been drawn ; if from the manufacturing, the fame muft take place, in order that the proportion of the ftock in each employment may be preferved, confiftently with the actual ftate of the fociety with refpect to the quantity on the whole. But it has been afferted, that as the ftock is confumed within the fociety, it cannot be of any differvice; we fhall, however, fee the abfurdity of fuch an opinion, on obferving the manner in which it is fpent by government, and that in which it would be difpofed of, had it remained in the hands of the individual. In the former cafe, it is confumed in employing workmen in making the implements of war, in building fhips, in providing cloathing and provifions for the troops; all of which are confumed, without a poffibility of reproduction. In the latter cafe, that is, when employed by the individual, it is confumed by workmen who produce commodities which are again diftributed, and replaced by the produce of the labourer. In the firft cafe, it totally difappears; in the fecond, as it is confumed it is replaced.

If

If we faw a man employed, one day, in piling up a heap of ſtones which he threw down the next, we ſhould ſay, his employment was a uſeleſs one, although it might perhaps be as fatiguing as that of others, or though he was equally attentive; and it would certainly be very abſurd for any one to ſay, that he was of as much ſervice to ſociety as the farmer or manufacturer: but what real difference is there between the employment of ſuch a perſon, and that of one who is employed in making gun-powder, for the purpoſe of being exploded, or the other articles conſumed in a manner not more uſeful to ſociety. The idea, becauſe conſumption is confined to a particular nation, it cannot be injurious, is the moſt abſurd, and it would be happy for mankind if we had it not in our power to add, the moſt ruinous idea ever received by men. Are extravagance and œconomy, words ſo well known in common life, without meaning; they both ſuppoſe conſumption; yet why, if every ſpecies of conſumption be the ſame, do we annex ideas of ruin to the one and proſperity to the other?

The funding ſyſtem, therefore, by no means prevents the conſumption of ſtock. The capital ſtock of the country, on which the employment of labour and every ſpecies of revenue depends, would not be more reduced, if a tax were raiſed amounting to the whole of the ſum neceſſary for

the

the extraordinary expence. The only difference would be, that the stock of each person would be somewhat reduced, in place of many people giving up the whole and receiving a certain sum per annum on it. Under each suppofition, the number of labourers which the stock could employ, and the annual produce, would be precisely the same. But the effects of the funding system is not confined to the reduction of the national stock, as the imposition of an annual tax becomes necessary, in order to pay the interest on the sum borrowed. The effects of taxes, in keeping down the rate of wages and of profit, and thereby preventing the advance of the society, in population and in wealth, we have already shewn; these dreadful effects are, therefore, to be laid to the account of this system. It should be considered, as not only reducing the capital stock of the country, but also preventing the part which remains from accumulating as fast as it otherwise would do. It is therefore doubly destructive, and the injury, which it does in the former way, is but trifling, compared with that which it does in the latter. The amount of the original debt is by no means so great, as the sums which have been paid as interest on it. If, therefore, the expences of the state had been paid by a direct tax, the whole of what has been paid, as interest, would have been saved, and added to the wealth

of

of the country. Wages of labour muſt have been greater, which would have enabled the lower claſſes to have reared up more numerous families. We have, therefore, to lament the loſs of a vaſt number of people, as well as a vaſt quantity of wealth. This ſyſtem is unjuſt and partial: it falls particularly hard on the lower orders. By the diminution of the ſtock, they are thrown out of employment, or compelled to take leſs wages, and by taxes a part of the miſerable pittance which remains, is taken from them; nor is this abſurd and ruinous ſyſtem of any advantage to the owners of ſtock, except for the moment: it leaves them the whole of their ſtock, but reduces their profits. If they look to what may take place within 8 or 10 years, they may ſay the funding ſyſtem is of advantage to them. If they look to the intereſt of their children, they will perceive it hurtful. If they look to the intereſt of their grand children, they will perceive it ruinous. If a man believe he will live but a few years, he will prefer giving up a part of his profit, to ſecure the whole amount of his ſtock; becauſe he may encroach on it; but if he be ſure of living for a conſiderable number of years, he will prefer to ſacrifice part of his ſtock, to ſecure a large profit; becauſe, it would be folly in him to conſume any part of his capital. But when we look

to national benefit, to which private advantage
fhould always yield, in what terms can the baneful effects of this fyftem be expreffed? In a
a word, had the real effects of it been known,
when it was introduced, it fhould have been ftil-
ed, an infamous combination of the rich, againft
the poor and againft pofterity.

Let for a moment be conceived the fituation
of Great Britain, if the expences of her former
wars had been paid by direct taxes, the whole of
the enormous fums raifed on the people, in time
even of profound peace, would have been altogether unneceffary; it would be added to her
wealth, and fhe would have carried on the war, in
which fhe is at prefent engaged, with a fum confiderably lefs than that neceffary for the fupport
of the government in time of peace. If, during
the progrefs of her enormous debts, we have feen
her advance in wealth and power confiderably
fafter than the other nations of Europe; what
would be her prefent fituation, if fhe had been
totally freed from them, or if the expences
of her wars had been paid by taxes immediately impofed? Even during the American war, the moft expenfive fhe ever waged,
fhe was not reduced in wealth; as the favings of
individuals more than overbalanced the expences
of the government; happy if thefe expences, by

being

being raifed immediately from the people, had drawn on no other.

In the prefent war, the fame fyftem is purfued; the confumption of capital, attended by the taxing of the capital that remains: whatever the wealth and revenues of Great Britain be fuppofed, if under the preffure of the law of entail, by which 12 millions are annually confumed, and her taxes amounting together to about 30 millions, fhe advanced but flowly, it is eafy to fee, that a further confumption of more than 20 millions annually, together with the intereft on it, muft either ftop her altogether, or rather put her back: to this we are to add the interruption of her commerce, and the great number of her fhips captured by the enemy, the unavoidable concomitants of wars.

In the nation to which fhe is oppofed, we fee another fyftem totally different adopted; we fee the emiffion of paper money to an amount fcarcely conceivable, and its confequent depreffion. In judging of the actual expences of France, we muft firft look to the neceffary confequence of increafing the quantity of money in circulation. It appears matter of furprize in France, that their affignats fhould be depreciated, as the value of the national lands, which may be deemed a fufficient fecurity, is confiderably greater than the whole amount of the affignats in circulation.

circulation. It was never expected that assignats should ever serve any other purpose than that of circulation, or that they had any particular virtue in them above the money which they are intended to supply. We have shewn, however, that even money, when increased to a certain degree, must fall in its value, and exactly in proportion to the extraordinary quantity. Every person possessed of money, or any thing serving as money, as the assignats of France, must, in order to dispose of it to advantage, put it into circulation; and as we have formerly observed, the value of each portion must depend on the quantity of the whole. It would be as absurd to suppose, that commodities should bear the same value, after the quantity of money was increased, as that a man in a desart could convert, at pleasure, a shilling into a shilling loaf. If 5 men go to market with 5 shillings each, and there be at market goods of the value of 25 shillings, each person may procure goods of the value of 5 shillings; but if one person should convert his 5 shillings into 10 or 15, if he purchase goods at the old price, none will remain for some of the rest; but all going to market together, and each wishing to procure as much as possible, it must lower the value of each portion of money; or, what amounts to the same thing, raise the value of the goods. Unless, therefore, it can be demonſtrated, that individuals have a greater intereſt in hoarding aſſignats than ſpecie, their value muſt fall as the quantity increaſes. Had the convention of France a treaſure of gold and ſilver at command, it muſt have preciſely the ſame effect, if, as their aſſignats are, it could be kept within the country; but being the ſtandard of value in other countries, it would be carried out, when it had affected the nominal value of of goods in general.

Thus, by the emiſſion of aſſignats, we ſee the ſtandard of value totally altered, we ſee it affect the nominal value of every ſpecies of goods; are we juſtified then in computing the expences of France, by money which no longer retains the ſame value? We muſt look to things, and not to ſounds: the expences of a nation are either great or ſmall, as a greater or ſmaller portion of the annual revenue is conſumed. If, in Great Britain, it was enacted, that each ſhilling ſhould be called a pound, and each pound a ſhilling, we ſhould ſay our expences ſince the commencement of the war have amounted to 70 millions of ſhillings, or 1400 millions of pounds, but the real expences would ſtill be the ſame, the ſame portion of the national ſtock conſumed.

The expences, therefore, of the French government, are by no means to be eſtimated by the number of livres, unleſs we apply a certain

determinate

determinate idea to the value of each livre, determined by the quantity of confumable commodities which it can command; and this it is evident is no longer the fame.

The quantity of money, neceffary for the circulation of France, before the war, it is generally fuppofed, was equivalent to 90 millions fterling. In the month of December, the total of their expences amounted to 503,478,000 livres, about £22,000,000. there were then upwards of 10,000,000,000 in circulation, about £437,500,000; they muft, therefore, have been reduced nearly as low as one fifth; their expences then muft have amounted to 4 millions and a half. Were we to fuppofe the war to continue, for fome years longer, at the fame real expence to France, we fhould fee it as reprefented in affignats rife to an incredible amount; but every time the quantity in circulation is doubled, we are not to fuppofe that the confumption has been equal to the quantity of money which had originally ferved the purpofe of circulation; that is, when the quantity at prefent in circulation, about 10,000,000,000 is increafed to 20,000,000,000, that their expences have amounted to 90 millions fterl. the fum formerly neceffary for circulation; at moft it cannot amount to more than 67 millions and a half. For, in our chapter on money, we have fhewn, that as the quantity in circulation is increased, the value of each portion is gradually reduced; thus, if 20 millions be introduced into a country that has 20 millions in circulation, the last million brought in can procure but half the quantity of goods that the first did, as the nominal value of goods must be raised to nearly twice that which they had formerly borne.

The real effects of the emission of assignats are, first, the rise of every species of goods and of revenue, but a greater rise in the price of goods than of revenue. If goods and revenue were raised together, in the same proportion, things would be exactly as they were; but the rise of revenue is in consequence of the rise in the value of goods, by the constant emission of assignats: the one must necessarily go *before* the other. The greater rise in the value of goods than of revenue, must be determined by the quantity of assignats issued to purchase the goods necessary for the consumption of the armies, fleets, &c. of France. This is the tax paid by the people. To elucidate this important subject a little more fully. If we suppose the money in France turned three times a year, (whether faster or slower is of no importance to our supposition) that is, in 4 months 10,000 millions of assignats appear for the purchase of goods, if within these four months no assignats be issued by government, the whole of the

the goods at market will be diftributed to the workmen, manufacturers, merchants, landholders, &c. and there will appear but 10,000 millions during the four months following; but if the expences of the ftate amount to 2000 millions of livres, as reprefented in affignats, they muft come, at market, in competition with the 10,000 millions, and the goods which had fold in the one cafe for 10,000, would then fell for 12,000; that is, while the money which reprefented the revenue of each perfon remained ftationary, goods had been raifed in their value; but the additional 2000, now becomes the property of the different orders of fociety, and are diftributed amongft them; the merchant muft give a greater price to the manufacturer for his goods, the manufacturer muft give greater wages to his workmen; and thus the next four months, 12,000 millions of livres reprefent the revenues of the different orders: but, during thefe four months, the expences of government, although really the fame, muft be reprefented by a greater quantity of affignats: to procure the fame quantity of goods 2400 millions become neceffary. Thus we difcover the manner in which the emiffion of affignats affects the revenues of France.

It will be readily feen, that this is a moft equitable mode of defraying the public expence, as the proportion which each perfon contributes is determined by the abundance of his revenue. Both profits of ftock and wages of labour are taxed, and each exactly in the proportion that they ought. The diminution of profit, which prevents accumulation, is attended by a diminution of wages, which prevents the lower orders from multiplying.

Whether the taxes, thus raifed, together with the confumption of the country, exceed the amount of their foil, labour, and ftock, is not very doubtful. If the expences of Great Britain (allowing nothing for the law of entail, which is now done away in France) in peace, amounted to upwards of 17 millions fterl. and under this load fhe advanced, though but flowly, it is fcarcely poffible, that the confumption of about 55 millions annually, under the prefent circumftances of of France, when we confider the vaft extent and wealth of the countries from which fhe at prefent derives a revenue, will oblige her to encroach on her ftock. But although this became neceffary, the confumption of the ftock of France would be attended by none of thofe dreadful effects that it muft be in England. By the emiffion of affignats, a tax is raifed directly on the revenues of the people; if this, together with their confumption, exceed the annual amount of the revenue, a certain portion only of the ftock is confumed, consumed, the part which remains is left unloaded. In England, however, a part of the stock is directly consumed; in all her former wars, when she was not so much encumbered by annual taxes, the savings of individuals, from their revenues, more than overbalanced the consumption of stock: but the power of accumulating is always directly prevented by the annual taxes, which, under the system at present pursued, are unavoidable. When, therefore, in Great Britain the annual expences exceed the annual income, she is not only obliged to consume part of her stock, but the part which remains is prevented from being increased. When the remaining stock becomes insufficient to pay the interest of debts, formerly contracted, it must be broken in on, to pay even the interest. Whenever this takes place, unless a bankruptcy, by ruining a few thousands, should save the nation, she must quickly fall to decay[*]. In nations, as in France, where the annual expences are directly paid out of the annual revenues, and if that be not sufficient, directly paid from the stock; the decline, if such enormous expences be continued, must be gradual; but the moment they cease, individuals are soon enabled to make up their losses, by their profits being left unloaded.

[*] We shall at a future period offer some observations on the most adviseable means of redeeming public debts.

Of all the taxes which human ingenuity could devise, those obtained by the emission of paper money are, when well understood, the least destructive. It is liable to but one objection; the possibility of forgeries. The convention of France appears, however, to have been totally ignorant of its real nature, when it adopted the unjust and impolitic law of the maximum. Commodities should be allowed to find their own value; and, of all commodities, food is the most dangerous to tamper with. The natural rate of food, as well as of other commodities should rise in proportion to the quantity of assignats in circulation. This, experience has demonstrated.

When the real effects of the emission of paper money are understood, we will see the necessity of laws, in order to prevent too great a share of the public burthens from falling on a few individuals. A law, to regulate the payment of debts, rents, &c. appears to be one of these. If an individual contract a debt, at a certain time, he may pay the same debt at a distant day with the same sum in paper money, but which, in consequence of the increased quantity, may bear a very different value. This, it behoves every government to guard against, by fixing the value of the paper money; that is, determining what quantity of it should exchange for a certain quantity of

specie

specie, which should be always considered as the standard.

After treating of the immediate effects of the emission of paper money, it will be necessary to call our attention to the manner in which the circulation of a country may be freed from it, after a further emission becomes unnecessary. We shall first offer some arguments which are applicable to France, in common with other countries, and then consider the nature of the peculiar circumstances under which she is placed.

It will be readily seen, that a sum, in specie, equal to the amount of that which had formerly served for circulation, can at all times command the whole mass of paper money, at its reduced value. Thus taxes, to half the amount of the expences of the old government of France, would, in little more than 5 years, free the circulation of the whole of the assignats. For if 90 millions were necessary, when the people were oppressed by the law of entail, and the great annual taxes; it would scarcely require more than 60 or 70, under the circumstances in which France will be placed at the termination of the war. These taxes may be paid either in specie, or assignats received at their reduced rate. If in assignats, they should be immediately destroyed. If in specie, a quantity of assignats should be purchased with it, and also destroyed. Or, the circulation

tion may be freed from them, by making a forcible and gradual depreſſion of their value; that is, by altering, at different times, the relative value between ſpecie and aſſignats, and at length prohibiting their being received in any ſpecies of payment. The objection to the former mode is, chiefly, the neceſſity of any ſpecies of tax, above that neceſſary for the ſupport of the ſtate. The objections to the latter, are the difficulty of making the depreſſion in ſuch a manner as that each individual ſhall be affected, in proportion to his wealth, precifely in the ſame degree, and the interruption which commerce muſt ſuffer, in conſequence of the artifices and frauds of certain individuals. It muſt conſequently be, for theſe reaſons, more odious, and as the ultimate effects of both are alike, that ſyſtem ſhould be adopted under which every perſon knows to what he has to truſt. Every country, which purſues this mode of defraying the extraordinary public expences, will have to purchaſe from the other nations, the money neceſſary for its circulation, which the emiſſion of paper money drives out. When a further emiſſion becomes unneceſſary, and it is reſolved to call in all the paper, its value ſhould be fixed, determined by the quantity in circulation; that is, as in France, whether one livre in ſpecie ſhall be worth 5, 10, or 15 in paper. When any part is withdrawn from circulation,

tion, if the remainder be kept at its reduced value, (which ought to be done,) it, together with the fpecie already in the country, will be infufficient for the circulation. The nominal value of goods muſt fall, as the reduced quantity of paper at the reduced value, together with the fpecie, muſt command the goods at market. It muſt therefore become the intereſt of people to carry money in, and goods out, until the whole of the paper is withdrawn from circulation, and the nominal value of goods on a level with thofe in other countries. If the value of the paper be reduced by law, without withdrawing any from circulation, the fame will take place, as in both cafes the value of fpecie is raifed fomewhat higher than it is in other countries.

Although government, in withdrawing paper money from circulation, by the impofition of taxes, commands or receives no part of the annual produce, yet it has precifely the fame effect on the revenues of the people, as a tax to the fame amount, in countries where the circulation is carried on by means of fpecie. By deſtroying a part of the paper money, a gap is made, which muſt be filled up by money from other countries; and thus, in place of the people giving up a portion of their revenues to the government, they give it to foreign nations: fo that the effects are precifely fimilar. In the firſt emiffion of paper

per money, the specie is driven out, and goods are carried in, so that the expences of wars are not felt, until the whole of the money is carried out, and the further emission of paper deprives the people of part of the produce of their labour; and on the other hand, the expences are felt, while the specie which had at first been driven out by the paper money, is carried in from other countries.

A law may reduce the value of paper money, when compared with that of specie, although it cannot raise it. Thus, if the natural value of assignats be one fifth, in consequence of the quantity in circulation, it may be reduced to one tenth, by enacting that they should not be received in taxes, but at the reduced rate, or considered as a legal tender in payment of debts, &c. it must then become the interest of people to carry money into the country, as the assignats, at their reduced value, would be insufficient for circulation: but if there was a law, that 5 livres in assignats should exchange for 5 in specie, it could have no other effect, than to send all the specie out of the country, as it must be of five times the value in any other.

As specie cannot, for any length of time, bear a lower value in one country than another, it must be evident, that if the circulation of a country, in which there exists a necessity of the emission of
paper

paper money, be partly compofed of fpecie, that the value of the paper may be lower, than if the fpecie was entirely driven out. If, for example, the circulation of France required 90 millions fterling, and there were affignats to the amount of 90, and fpecie to 45 millions, the value of the affignats would be half that of the fpecie Hence we fee the neceffity of very fevere laws, to prevent the depreciation of the paper money. It is true, thefe laws can never raife the value of paper to a level with that of fpecie, the moment there is in circulation, a quantity of paper, greater than the money which had originally ferved all the purpofes of circulation; but thefe laws can force the fpecie out of the country, and thereby prevent the paper from being ftill further depreciated. If individuals were allowed to receive paper money, at a very reduced value, or refufe it altogether, a very fmall part of the money would be carried out; nor could the public expence be paid in this manner. When government is not under a neceffity of iffuing any more paper money, a fimple permiffion to allow the people to receive it at any rate they pleafed, would alone be fufficient, in the courfe of a fhort time, to put it out of circulation.

But, as in France, the value of the confifcated lands, is great enough to allow the purchafe of the affignats at their full value; we fhall now examine

the

the policy of freeing the circulation, by means of the fale of thefe lands. It will firft, however, be neceffary, to offer fome obfervations on the nature of the capital value of land. Profits of ftock, which regulate the intereft of money, will be found to regulate the value of land alfo. A man, in difpofing of his money, will be fatisfied with a fmaller fum per cent. if he purchafe lands with it, than if he lend it on intereft; becaufe it is better fecured, and he derives other advantages from it: but thefe are equivalent to a certain difference only; whatever, therefore, reduces the profits of ftock, raifes the capital value of lands: and this, as we have already fhewn, is done by the law of entail and annual taxes. Moreover, when, after the divifion of the lands, the accumulation of ftock is fuch, that the price of the produce is little more than fufficient, to fecure to the cultivator the ordinary profits, the capital value of land muft be confiderably reduced. But, as in France, the value of the confifcated lands is yet confiderable, in confequence of this divifion not having taken place, and the interruptions which agriculture fuffers; and as the perfon who can obtain any part of them, muft receive a revenue greater than he is entitled to from his labour or ftock; we fhall point out the effects of redeeming the affignats, by the fale of thefe lands, on the feveral orders of fociety.

We

We have already feen that, in the emiffion of affignats, each order contributes its proper proportion to the expences of the ſtate. We are then to conſider, if each order would be benefited in the ſame degree, if the affignats were purchaſed by the ſale of the lands. If we ſuppoſe the value of the lands juſt equal to the affignats in circulation, at their full value, and each perſon to receive a quantity of land, in proportion to the quantity of affignats in his hands, the diſtribution would be extremely partial. It is generally ſuppoſed, that the quantity of money neceffary for circulation, may amount to about one fourth or one fifth of the annual revenue. Now, as the lower orders have never more than half their week's wages, on an average, in their hands, the remainder of the money muſt neceſſarily be in the hands of the other orders. Each citizen, having contributed his proper ſhare to the public expence, during the emiffion of the paper money, it would appear that each muſt naturally have an equal claim on the public lands. But if they be diſtributed in this way, the lower orders would receive lands, (or what amounts to the ſame thing, the value of lands, as they might be ſold for their benefit,) to the amount of half their weekly wages, while the other orders would receive lands, to the value of one fourth or one third of their yearly revenue; we ſay one fourth or one third, becauſe as much

as

as the lower orders have in hand, less than their share of the money in circulation, in proportion to their annual revenue, the other orders must have more. But although one order had no greater proportion of their annual revenue in hand than another, it would still be a very partial division. If the wages of the workmen be, for 4 months, £9, and the profit of the manufacturer for the same period, £90; and if, in consequence of the emission of a large quantity of paper money, the former be represented by £45, and the latter by £450, and there be lands to the value of £495 in specie, to be divided, to which each, as an individual, has an equal right, it would certainly be a very unfair mode of division, if the manufacturer were to receive 11 times the quantity which fell to the share of the workman. The lands are of a much greater value than what has been really expended by the republic; for the manufacturer who now advances 5 livres, nominally, to government, really advances but one, as the paper money is so much reduced in value; the same with the labourer*. If the assignats, therefore, be purchased by government

---

* Since the above was written, the quantity of assignats has been considerably increased, attended by a very great depreciation of their value. The reader, therefore, must receive the above, and many of the suppositions which follow, only as illustrations of the general principle.

at

at their full value, it will not only repay individuals what they have really advanced, but considerably more. The manufacturer, who nominally advances 50, and really but 10, will receive 40 more than he has advanced; while the labourer, who has advanced 5 nominally, and really but 1, receives but 4. Under every fuppofition, the withdrawing affignats from circulation, by the fale of the lands, muft be impolitic and partial. There appears, therefore, but one way, by which the lower orders can derive any advantage from the confifcated lands, that is by felling them, and giving to each perfon the fhare of the produce. But this, though poffible would be extremely impolitic, and would be attended by very fatal effects, even to the poor. The ftock which the individual would give for the land, would be directly divided amongft the lower orders, and moft probably confumed: they muft then, neceffarily, be in a worfe fituation, than if it had been left in the hands of the original owners, and the lands given away, in place of being fold; as the ftock which remained muft be infufficient to afford them employment. Confidered in any point of view, it would be highly impolitic, for although there were fome, who had forefight fufficient to prevent them from confuming it, they muft in order to derive any advantage from it, work independently of employers: but this, in moft employments, is

altogether

altogether impoffible, as extenfive works and large ftocks are abfolutely neceffary.

Thus we may perceive, that the confifcated lands are really of but little affiftance to France. Had the original owners retained poffeffion of them, its force might have been precifely the fame. There remains then a queftion to be decided, in what manner can thefe extenfive lands be difpofed of, fo as that they fhall be of the greateft poffible fervice to every defcription of men? We have already pointed out the advantages of the lands being divided into fuch portions, as lay their owners under the neceffity of cultivating them, but the way in which this may beft be done, is what we have no bufinefs to offer an opinion of.

We are now enabled to form a judgement of the comparative ftate of the finances of France and Great Britain. The annual expences of the former, amount to about 55 millions fterling*, which will ceafe at the termination of

---

* We have here eftimated their expences by thofe of December: there were, however, even then, fome fpecie and forged affignats in circulation, and confequently their real expences muft have been much lefs. Since that time, jobbing, and the introduction of an immenfe quantity of forged affignats and fpecie have greatly depreciated thofe iffued by the government. We muft always, however, judge of their real expences, by the degree of this depreciation; and at which, whatever it be, they fhould be redeemed.

the war; thofe of the latter, amount to more than 20 millions of annual taxes, and about the fame fum in ftock, to which if we add the foreign loan, which muft be confidered as a further confumption of ftock, the whole will amount to about 45 millions. We fee France in the prefent conteft, deriving her revenues from a country about 4 times as rich and populous as Great Britain, and the whole of thefe revenues directed to one object. We fee Great Britain with refources fo much inferior, at nearly the fame expence; but her revenues are not like thofe of France, directed wholly to the fupport of the war, but a great part to the payment of the intereft on the debts contracted in the wars in which fhe has been engaged for this century. It does not require the gift of prophecy, to foretel the confequences of perfevering in this ruinous conteft.

CHAP. XIX.

Wealth.

ALTHOUGH, from what we have already said, the nature of wealth may be sufficiently understood, yet it may, perhaps, be not altogether unnecessary to add a few more observations. As civilized society is not a society of farmers, or merchants, or labourers, but a whole, of which each is a part; so shall we find, what is generally styled the wealth of such a society, composed of parts, the uses and value of which depend not so much on their own nature, as on the relations which they bear to each other.

Wealth is of three kinds, lands, houses, stock; the latter is divided into fixed stock, or contrivances for abridging labour, and consumable commodities. These commodities are the revenues of the citizens, but are considered by their owners, only, as a source of revenue. It will naturally follow then, as the goods which constitute stock and revenue are precisely the same, and both bear a nominal value, that the proportion of the annual produce, which the possession of these commodities give to certain people; or, in

other

other words, high or low profits, will regulate what is commonly called the capital value of other fources of revenue; that is, when certain lands or houfes yield a certain revenue, their capital value will be either high or low, as profits of ftock are high or low. We fpeak of the capital value of land, as a thing in exiftence; it would, however, be juft as rational to fpeak of the capital value of a penfion, if it was allowed to be fold, as abfolutely exifting. A capital value is laid on certain things, for mere convenience, becaufe individuals frequently wifh to exchange the fubject, from which they derive a revenue, for another; fome men are fond of employment, others of eafe: but it is the revenue that is exchanged, and if one be greater than the other, it is always fuppofed compenfated by other circumftances: hence the rife of rent, in a twofold way, affects the value of land. If rent could be raifed, without affecting the profits of ftock, a rife in value would naturally take place; but as every rife of rent fuppofes a fall of profit, the value of the land muft be raifed in a ftill greater degree. We have faid the capital value of houfes is alfo regulated by the profits of ftock. The rent which a houfe affords, is not always regulated by the quantity of ftock which had been expended in building it, and the moment it is erected, whatever have been the expences, its capital value, which

may

may be termed its *exchangeable value*, muſt be determined by the rent. Every ſpecies of fixed ſtock, alſo, derives its value from the ſame ſource. Revenue, therefore, or the regular return of commodities, can alone give a value to every thing that is not commodities. If theſe be taken away, houſes, lands, fixed ſtock, all loſe their value; as in place of that application of labour, from which ultimately, though ſlowly, a great production ariſes, men would be compelled to ſeek for immediate ſubſiſtence, in the produce of immediate labour.

In the progreſs of wealth, we have ſhewn the progreſs of population, and the circumſtances which determine a greater or ſmaller proportion of the ſtock of the ſociety, to the different employments. When the market for the productions of every part of the country is moſt extenſive, *cæteris paribus*, a greater proportion to the mercantile; when the ſociety is advancing faſteſt in wealth and population, *cæteris paribus*, a greater proportion to agriculture, and the uſeful manufactures.

The reader, however, muſt recollect, that though this is the natural order, in which ſtock is diſtributed amongſt the ſeveral employments, yet that, in every ſociety, in conſequence of regulations, (the effects of which will make part of the ſubject of a future work,) this natural diſtribution of ſtock

stock is prevented. It will be abfolutely neceſſary for us, therefore, to remark the relations in which different countries ſtand to each other. A favourite ſyſtem takes place in all; ſome encourage agriculture, others commerce and manufactures, but ſtill the general principles hold. The ſtock of Great Britain, may be the manufacturing and mercantile ſtock of America; the ſtock of America, the farming ſtock of Great Britain; but ſtill ſtock, in the ſeveral employments, whether in France, in Great Britain, America, or Spain, muſt bear certain relations to each other, determined by the circumſtances already pointed out.

In the XIVth Chapter, we have ſhewn the effects of credit, only, as it relates to a particular country; but when long credits are given by the merchants and manufacturers of one country to thoſe of another, ſtock becomes in reality employed for the advantage of the latter. It has been aſſerted, and with truth, that the population of Great Britain has not kept pace with its wealth: great part of her ſtock is employed as the mercantile ſtock of other countries, and in p'ace of contributing to the increaſe of people in Great Britain, contributes in a great degree to the population of America and other countries, to the merchants of which ſuch long credits are granted; thus, allowing a greater proportion of ſtock to remain

remain in the farming and manufacturing employments, on which workmen are more immediately dependent.

CHAP. XX.

Recapitulation and Conclusion.

I. IN societies, where the inhabitants are more numerous than the spontaneous produce of the lands can maintain, the commodities at a certain moment consumed, never arise wholly from the labour at that moment employed.

II. In every society, there must be a quantity of every species of commodities sufficient for its consumption, until those of the same kind can be produced.—The quantity of corn got in at time of harvest, must be sufficient for consumption until the return of the next.

III. No society being confined, in its consumption, to its own productions, with part of which it purchases the produce of others, a quantity of commodities, becomes necessary, sufficient for consumption, until those produced in foreign countries can be procured.——Although sugar be purchased with part of the produce of England,
yet

yet fugar does not immediately follow the production of thofe goods, with which it is purchafed. There muft, therefore, be not only commodities fufficient for the confumption of thofe employed on thefe goods, but a quantity of fugar fufficient for confumption until more can be procured.

IV. As labour is not rewarded by its immediate produce, it will follow, that the number of people will always be dependent on the quantity of commodities exifting within the fociety, and that an increafe of commodities muft always go *before* an increafe of people.——The infant eats and is clothed, but produces nothing.

V. It is impoffible for an increafe of population to take place, unlefs labour be employed in agriculture and the ufeful manufactures: but as a town may increafe in population without agriculture, becaufe of its connection with the country in its neighbourhood, fo may a fociety, even though employed in the production of articles of luxury, provided thofe articles are fent to others, for the purchafe of the produce of agriculture; and fo may a fociety be ftationary, even though employed in agriculture, fhould it purchafe with its produce articles of luxury. This points out the relation in which different countries, or parts of the fame country, may ftand to each other. The general propofition is ftill, however, true, that agriculture and the ufeful manufactures muft

be

be attended to, in order to allow an increafe of people. The increafe of men, in a favage ftate, is limited by the fpontaneous produce of the foil; in civilized fociety, by the proportion of labour ufefully employed. Nature in the one cafe, man in the other, is the nurfe of the rifing generation.

VI. The commodities within the fociety, (II. III.) are the revenue of that fociety, until others are produced or procured. That the confumption cannot exceed this quantity, is evident, and that the confumption fhall be equal to it, is fecured by the intereft of thofe poffeffed of them.

VII. Thefe commodities are diftributed amongft three orders; thofe poffeffed of them, as farmers, manufacturers, and merchants, the owners of the land, and the labouring part of the community. As the confumption of one order is raifed, that of another muft, confequently, be diminifhed.

VIII. The family which the labouring man is able to maintain, will depend on the rate of his wages. In countries, therefore, advancing in population, the proportion of the commodities, diftributed as wages, will bear a greater, that as profit and rent, a fmaller proportion, to the whole mafs of commodities within the fociety. But the abfolute quantity diftributed to each order, will depend on the fertility of the foil and the divifion of labour.

IX.

IX. The commodities which the lower orders confume, are of a different fpecies from thofe confumed by the others. In focieties, therefore, where the wages of labour are high, there will exift (XIX.) and be a demand for more of the produce of agriculture, and the ufeful manufactures, than in thofe where they are low, and confequently a greater proportion of labour and ftock will be employed in their production. (V.)

X. The quantity of commodities confumed within a given period, ought to be regulated by the quantity exifting, and the time before others can be produced or procured. (XIV.)

XI. After the divifion of employments has been eftablifhed, as no individual is employed on all the articles of his confumption, nor confumes the whole of his own produce, barter or a circulating medium becomes neceffary, in order to fupply himfelf by exchange. But barter muft, in a fhort time, give place to a medium, as innumerable articles go through the hand of hundreds, before they are finifhed, and confequently before they acquire an exchangeable value with confumers*.

XII. The circulating medium which appears for the purchafe of goods, within a certain period,

---

* Even the ancient Britons, according to Cæfar, ufed a circulating medium. "Utuntur (fays he) aut æreo, aut taleis ferreis, ad certum pondus examinatis, pro nummo."

will depend on the quantity of the whole, and the slowness or fastness with which it passes through the hands of the several orders.

XIII. The quantity of the goods which must be sold, within a certain period, will depend on the quantity of the whole, and the length of time before others can be procured.

XIV. The circulating medium is of no advantage to those possessed of it, unless they employ it, and in whatever way we conceive it employed, it must *ultimately* go to the purchase of goods. Commodities are of no advantage to those possessed of them, unless by giving them the power over others by barter or by their sale. The circulating medium, therefore, cannot be held up, but with a view of purchasing cheaper; nor commodities, but to be sold dearer: but whether the circulating medium shall command more goods, or goods more of the circulating medium, will depend on the quantity, &c. (XII.) of the former, which must ultimately go to the purchase of goods, and the quantity, &c. (XIII.) of the latter, which must ultimately be sold.

XV. The circulating medium may be produced within the society, or purchased from another. If a production of the society serve as the circulating medium, when the profits of those employed on it are on a level with those in other employments, the quantity of labour and stock, which may be engaged with the common advantages, can never be more than fufficient to replace the regular confumption; that is, when thofe who employ themfelves in the production of commodities can command as much of the circulating medium, by their fale, as if they had employed themfelves directly in its production*. If procured from another fociety, the advantages which may be derived from its purchafe will depend, as in the former cafe, on the value of that in circulation; that is, whether goods can command more of the circulating medium by being difpofed of abroad than at home.

XVI. When paper is introduced into circulation, there is a relation eftablifhed between it and the medium, but not between paper and commodities, and by coming into circulation, and commanding goods as well as the medium, it necefsarily reduces its value, (XII. XIV.) If produced within the fociety, the employment of a fmaller quantity of labour and ftock will be found fufficient: if procured from another, people will be able to purchafe goods cheaper in other countries; a quantity, therefore, will be carried out, and goods carried in, or its import-

* The mines of Spain were formerly confidered fertile, and many had an intereft in working them, but fince the difcovery of America it has been found of greater advantage to produce commodities.

ation

ation for some time prevented, by this reduction in its value. Although the emission of paper gives the command of a greater proportion of the productions to certain people than they are entitled to, yet the saving which it occasions must be equal to it; this proportion cannot exceed the quantity of goods, in the one case, carried out, or which the emission prevents being carried out; nor, in the other, the additional quantity produced, in consequence of less labour and stock being employed in the production of the medium. The stock, on which the employment of labour depends, is augmented nearly the amount of the paper in circulation*.

XVII. When barter takes place, the revenues of the three orders are represented immediately in commodities; when a circulating medium is introduced, by its quantity; and in the latter case, as well as in the former, the quantity received by the one order, will determine the quantity to be given to the remaining.—Should the rise of rent, for example, be represented in the price of the materials of manufactures, wages and profit would be reduced in their nominal amount, and manufactures, taken in a mass, would sell for

---

* Bankers are under the necessity of keeping a quantity of specie on hands, which, however, cannot be, by any means, equal to the amount of their paper in circulation, their advantages being regulated by the difference.

precisely

precisely the same price; but as it falls also on the commodities immediately consumed, as provisions, &c. wages and profit must be reduced, partly really and nominally, by the rise of the materials of manufactures, and partly really, by the rise of the articles of immediate consumption; that is, the quantity of money received by workmen and the owners of stock would be reduced, and the price of certain articles raised. Manufactures would sell at the same price, (see Chap. VII. and note.)

XVIII. The exchangeable value of every article will depend on the demand for it and its quantity, not on the labour which has been employed in its production*.

XIX. The quantity of a commodity at market will depend on the labour and stock which have been employed in its production; and the quantity of labour and stock employed in the production of a certain commodity will depend on the exchangeable value of those of the same kind at

---

* There is a great demand for water, but it bears scarcely any exchangeable value, because so easily procured. The exchangeable value of provisions, in a town besieged, is not regulated by the labour and stock which had been employed in their production, nor of commodities when circumstances make it necessary to dispose of a greater quantity than for which there is a demand.

market.

market*. The quantity and species of commodities at market will consequently be of the kind for which there is a demand, if this remains without any deviation from its ordinary course.

XX. Demand may be defined the ability and wish to exchange one commodity for another, which exchange may be made either by barter or a circulating medium. Whatever, therefore, be the quantity of production, there will be a demand for the whole, provided it is of the right species.

XXI. In order that a society shall advance in population and wealth, great wages must be given to the lower orders, which supposes œconomy amongst the others, and the employment of stock and labour in agriculture and the useful manufactures; from great wages arises an increase in the population, and from the increased population a greater production. The increase of stock always going before and always followed by an increase of people; for as no increase of people can take place, unless preceded by an increase of stock; so no further increase of stock can take place, unless followed by that of people.

XXII. The productions arising from the increased population enters the hands of the own-

---

* The rent of land and taxes acts by raising the exchangeable value of commodities, without determining a greater quantity of labour and stock to their production.

ers of ſtock, in place of thoſe which had been advanced as wages, rent, and for their own conſumption, and what remains, after again advancing rent and the ordinary wages to the ſame number of workmen, is profit; part of which may be conſumed, part give employment to the additional number of workmen, which always follows high wages, and part may go to the augmentation of mercantile ſtock.

www.ingramcontent.com/pod-product-compliance
Lightning Source LLC
Chambersburg PA
CBHW031815220426
43662CB00007B/662